Learning Resources
for
Conducting Research

Social and Behavioral
Science Methods

Second Edition

Lawrence T. Orcher

with contributions by Danielle Dobies and Kyle Dump

Pyrczak Publishing
P.O. Box 250430 • Glendale, CA 91225

"Pyrczak Publishing" is an imprint of Fred Pyrczak, Publisher, A California Corporation.

Although the author and publisher have made every effort to ensure the accuracy and completeness of information contained in this book, we assume no responsibility for errors, inaccuracies, omissions, or any inconsistency herein. Any slights of people, places, or organizations are unintentional.

Contributing Author: Kyle Dump.
Editor: Danielle Dobies.

Cover design by Robert Kibler and Larry Nichols.

Learning Resource 2 prepared by Danielle Dobies.
Learning Resource 1 and 2 prepared by Kyle Dump.

Editorial assistance provided by Amber Avines, Wendy Baker, Kyle Dump, Joshua Leet, Janet Trakin, and Peggy Year.

Printed in the United States of America by McNaughton & Gunn, Inc.

Brief Contents

Notes:

Contents

Continued →

Introduction

Learning Resources for Conducting Research provides students with supplemental materials to achieve mastery in their study of research methods for the social and behavioral sciences.

Included in the *Learning Resources*

Learning Resource 1 is for students who are preparing a preliminary research proposal. By using the checklist, students will be reminded of every major step in preparing a proposal, as well as the proper sequence for the preparation of each part.

Learning Resource 2 provides an outline summary of each chapter. This resource should be used in two ways. First, students should read the summary of the chapter prior to reading the chapter itself. This is what is known as a *pre-reading activity*, which provides students with an overview of what they will be reading in a chapter. Pre-reading is widely believed to assist in comprehension while reading. Second, students will find it helpful to refer to the chapter outlines when preparing for examinations. When reading the chapter outlines for this purpose, students should ask themselves if they can discuss the meanings of the terms used in the outline and if they can give an example of each. Based on this exercise, students should know which particular terms and concepts they need to review in the textbook and in their classroom notes.

Learning Resource 3 provides an overview of major obstacles to conducting online research and the difficulties in interpreting research data gathered in this way. Practical solutions to issues with methods are provided. This is a "must read" for students planning online surveys.

The Binder Format

The three-hole binder format provides students with a convenient way to add notes for a variety of purposes as they progress through the course. For instance, when using *Learning Resource 1*, students may wish to add lined paper to make notes on their progress in preparing a preliminary research proposal. When using *Learning Resource 2*, students may want to add lined paper to make notes in class adjacent to the outline of the text, thus integrating the textbook material with the classroom presentations. *Learning Resource 3* describes a number of challenges to survey researchers. Students may want to keep notes on their progress in meeting these challenges.

Contacting the Author

I encourage you to share your criticisms of these learning resources with me. You can communicate with me via my publisher either through the mailing address shown on the title page or by sending an e-mail to Info@Pyrczak.com.

Lawrence T. Orcher
Los Angeles, California

Notes:

Learning Resource 1
Checklist for Preparing a Preliminary Research Proposal
(Based on Chapters 1 Through 11)

Directions: Below are the major steps for preparing a preliminary research proposal. For each step you take, place a checkmark on the line to its left. If a step does not apply to your proposal, write NA for "Not Applicable."

Chapter 1   Selecting Tentative Topics for Empirical Research

_____ Consider everyday observations as a source of research topics. Specifically, consider:

     _____ the prevalence of the observed behavior.

     _____ the demographics associated with the behavior.

     _____ the cause of the observed behavior.

     _____ what the observed behavior may cause.

     _____ whether it is possible to predict the behavior.

     _____ what theory or theories might account for the behavior.

_____ Stay open to more than one topic.

_____ Consider testing a theory by testing predictions derived from the theory.

_____ Make preliminary inquiries about the availability of participants.

_____ Avoid sensitive topics if you are a beginning researcher.

_____ Consult with instructors and members of your committee while selecting a topic.

_____ Scan journal articles for possible research topics. Specifically, consider conducting:

     _____ a modified replication based on a previous study's limitations.

     _____ a modified replication based on the researchers' insights.

_____ If your topic is too broad, consider narrowing it by using only one characteristic on a demographic variable (e.g., interview only male teachers).

_____ If it is too simple, consider adding one or more demographic variables. (e.g., interview teachers in Mexico as well as the United States to compare them).

Chapter 2   Locating Literature and Refining a Research Topic

_____ Decide which databases are likely to have research on tentative research topics. Some examples of places to look are:

     _____ PsycARTICLES

     _____ PsycINFO

     _____ ERIC

     _____ CSA Sociological Abstracts

     _____ Social Work Abstracts

     _____ Google Scholar

     _____ Consider other places specific to your topic.

_____ Use a citation index to find relevant research.

_____ Use a database thesaurus to find terms to use in a search.

_____ Use Boolean operators to refine a search.

_____ Search for theoretical literature to discuss in your literature review.
_____ Limit the search to the Title or Abstract fields for highly relevant articles.
_____ Consider searching for works by a particular author who has written on the topic.
_____ Look for relevant statistics at www.FedStats.gov.
_____ Keep a detailed record of how you conducted your search.
_____ Use a coding system while reading literature to make it easier to revisit later.
_____ Consider the literature when selecting and refining topics. Specifically, consider:
      _____ what demographics have been taken into account in previous research.
      _____ suggestions that previous researchers suggest for future research.

Chapter 3   Preparing a Literature Review

_____ Prepare a table that shows the key features of each article.
      _____ Give each article a unique identifier.
_____ Write an essay about the literature on your topic.
      _____ When writing an essay start by preparing a topic outline.
      _____ Include article identifiers for easy reference.
      _____ Note when particular articles might be cited at various points in the outline.
      _____ Note when multiple articles might be cited to support a single point.
_____ Name a specific topic near the beginning of the review.
_____ Cite statistics to establish the topic's importance near the beginning of the review.
_____ Write a critical review:
      _____ Avoid wording that makes all research seem equal in quality.
      _____ Consider indicating the quality of the individual studies cited.
      _____ Consider indicating your level of confidence in a group of research articles.
_____ Point out consistent findings in the literature.
_____ Point out gaps in the literature.
_____ Consider using subheadings in a long review.
_____ Describe relevant theories and how they relate to the topic.
_____ Point out the relationship between the literature review and the research question, purposes, or hypotheses.

Chapter 4   Citing References in APA and ASA Styles

_____ Make sure you know what style you are expected to use when writing.
_____ Familiarize yourself with the fundamentals of that style.
      _____ Obtain a copy of the APA Style Manual or ASA Style Guide for style specifics.

Chapter 5   Writing Research Hypotheses, Purposes, and Questions

_____ State your hypothesis near the end of the literature review.
      _____ Make sure your hypothesis does not state a value judgment.
      _____ If there are a number of hypotheses to be investigated, consider presenting them in a numbered list.
_____ If you want to explore a particular topic but are unable to predict the results, use a research purpose.
_____ Consider whether using a research question would better suit your topic.
_____ If a specific measure is the subject of your research, refer to it in the research hypotheses, purpose, or question.
_____ Consider writing several research hypotheses, purposes, or questions and asking for

feedback from instructors and other students.

Chapter 6   Selecting a Research Approach

_____   Consider what type of approach you will use.

_____   If you will use an experimental approach, identify at least one independent and one dependent variable.

_____   For a nonexperimental approach, consider using one of the following:

      _____   Causal-comparative research

      _____   Survey research

      _____   Correlational research

      _____   Document/content analysis

_____   Decide whether your topic lends itself to quantitative or qualitative research.

Chapter 7   Looking Ahead to Participant Selection

_____   Determine the number of participants used in published studies on your topic.

_____   Consider what type of sampling you will use to select a sample from a population.

      _____   Random sampling

      _____   Stratified sampling

      _____   Convenience sampling

      _____   Purposive sampling

Chapter 8   Looking Ahead to Measurement

_____   Consider using measures employed in previous research.

_____   Check the Test Collection Database to locate specialized measures.

_____   Consider if a match between the research goal and the measures can be improved greatly by devising a new measure.

_____   If conducting quantitative research, be sure to consider a measure's

      _____   validity.

      _____   reliability.

_____   If conducting qualitative research, be sure to consider a measure's credibility.

      _____   Consider if a measure uses member checks.

      _____   Consider if a measure uses prolonged engagement in the field.

      _____   Consider if a measure uses time sampling.

      _____   Make preliminary decisions on steps you might take to enhance the credibility of your measures.

_____   If conducting qualitative research, be sure to consider a measure's dependability.

      _____   Consider using multiple individuals to code and interpret the data.

      _____   Consider using a triangulation of measures.

Chapter 9   Looking Ahead to Data Analysis for Quantitative Research

_____   Analyze any nominal data.

      _____   Consider using percentages to analyze nominal data.

      _____   Use contingency tables when analyzing the relationship between two nominal variables.

      _____   Use a chi-square test to test the null hypothesis.

_____   Analyze group differences in interval variables.

      _____   Consider using means to study the differences between groups.

      _____   Describe the variability of a mean by using standard deviation.

_____ Use the *t* test to test the null hypothesis between two means.

_____ For more than two groups, use ANOVA to test the null hypothesis.

_____ Consider analyzing the change on interval variables by administering a pretest and a posttest.

_____ When examining the relationship between two interval variables, consider using the correlation coefficient.

Chapter 10   Looking Ahead to Data Analysis for Qualitative Research

_____ Make a preliminary, informal analysis of data while collecting data in qualitative research.

    _____ Consider writing memos in which you make notes of reactions and interpretations of data being collected.

    _____ Reflect on data as it is being collected and use your reflections as a basis for modifying questions, formulating additional questions, and even changing the line of questioning to obtain more useful data.

    _____ Consider collecting data from additional participants until you reach the point of data saturation.

_____ Consider using the Grounded Theory approach.

    _____ Open coding: Examine segments of the interview transcripts to identify distinct, separate segments. Then, code the individual segments to make them easier to identify.

    _____ Axial coding: Reexamine the transcripts of interviews and any other data sources to identify relationships between the categories identified during open coding.

    _____ Develop a core category.

_____ Consider using Hill's Consensual Qualitative Research approach.

    _____ Have members of a team work independently to identify domains.

    _____ Have the team members work together to reach a consensus on domains and core ideas.

    _____ Have the teams' work mediated by an auditor.

_____ Consider specific techniques for analysis of qualitative data by any approach.

    _____ Use enumeration to count how many respondents mentioned each important construct.

    _____ Select quotations to illustrate points made in the Results section.

    _____ Consider having two or more researchers code the data and consult with each other later to determine the extent to which their codes and interpretations are in agreement.

    _____ Consider diagramming the results.

    _____ Consider using peer debriefing.

    _____ Consider using auditing.

    _____ Consider conducting member checks.

    _____ Identify the range of responses.

    _____ Note and consider discrepant cases during data analysis for discrepant case analysis.

Chapter 11   Preparing a Preliminary Research Proposal

_____ Write a title for your proposal that is a brief statement that names major variables in the research hypothesis, purpose, or question. It may also indicate the specific types of participants studied.

_____ Consider adding the phrase "A Research Proposal" as a subtitle.

_____ Determine if you are expected to begin your proposal with an introduction followed by a separate literature review *or* to begin with an essay that integrates the two elements.

If the introduction is to be a separate essay, it should contain the following:

_____ Identification of the problem area

_____ Conceptual definitions of key terms

_____ An indication of why the topic is worthy of investigation, including the types of implications the results might have

_____ A brief description of any relevant theories, which should be expanded on in the literature review

_____ A statement of the specific research hypotheses, purposes, or questions the research is designed to explore

_____ For qualitative research, acknowledge that your personal perspectives may influence the interpretation of data.

_____ Include a "Method" section on your proposal.

_____ Include a subsection on "Participants" in the "Method" section.

_____ Consider starting the subsection with a description of the population from which the participants will be selected.

_____ Estimate the sample size.

_____ Provide a best guess as to the rate of participation.

_____ Describe the informed consent procedures you will use.

_____ Consider discussing any anticipated limitations in the selection of participants and how they might affect the results.

_____ Include a section on "Measures" in the "Method" section.

_____ Describe what type of measures will be used.

_____ Describe the types of demographics that will be collected.

_____ Consider interviewing participants using semi-structured or loosely structured interviews.

_____ Indicate the types of information that will be collected with the interviews.

_____ If you are using quantitative research, consider using objective-type measures to collect the data relating to the research's hypotheses, purposes, or questions.

_____ If new measures will be developed for use in the proposed research, make sure to describe them as specifically as possible.

_____ If there are important physical steps that will be taken in order to conduct the research that were not described under "Participants" and "Measures," discuss them under a subsection called "Procedures."

_____ Include an "Analysis" section in your proposal.

_____ Include a "Discussion" section where you summarize the proposal and discuss the limitations and strengths of the proposed study and possible implications.

_____ Include a list of "References" at the end of the proposal.

Notes:

Learning Resource 2

Chapter Outlines

These 27 chapter outlines provide important breakdowns of the topics covered and basic summaries of the main ideas covered in each topic. The outlines are intended to be used alongside the text as you work through each chapter. The outlines may also prove helpful for review when studying for an examination.

Notes:

Chapter 1: Selecting Tentative Topics for Empirical Research

I. Everyday Observations as a Source of Research Topics
    a) Especially useful when something unexpected is observed.
        (1) What is the prevalence of the observed behavior?
        (2) What are the demographics of those who exhibit the behavior?
        (3) What is the cause of the observed behavior?
        (4) What does the observed behavior cause?
        (5) Is it possible to predict the behavior?
        (6) What theory or theories might account for the behavior?

II. Theories as a Source of a Research Topic
    a) Consider predictions based on theories as possible topics for research.
    b) Research that supports the predictions supports the theories.
    c) Research results inconsistent with the predictions, dispute the theory.
    d) Because theories have many applications, research that contributes to theory building is generally held in higher regard than nontheoretical research.

III. Availability of Participants and Topic Selection
    a) Ideally, research topics are selected, narrowed before identifying participants.
    b) Because certain types of participants may be unavailable, make preliminary inquiries as to the availability of participants early.

IV. Ethical Considerations in Topic Selection
    a) Ethics require researchers to keep research participants free from physical and psychological harm.
    b) The mere act of asking certain questions might cause psychological distress.
    c) Beginning researchers should avoid sensitive topics.

V. The Audience's Expectations Regarding Topics
    a) Consult with instructors and members of a committee while selecting a topic. These individuals can help in a number of ways, such as:
        (1) Suggesting specific research topics within a student's area of interest.
        (2) Identifying barriers to conducting a satisfactory study on a given topic.
        (3) Helping to narrow a topic to make it more manageable.

VI. Personal Needs and Topic Selection
    a) It is acceptable to conduct research that can help meet certain personal needs as long as the researcher's involvement and feelings do not create blind spots.
    b) Avoid the urge to select a difficult or complex topic solely due to personal needs.

VII. Published Research as a Source of Topics
    a) Scan journal articles for ideas for research topics.
    b) While scanning, consider replicating a study:
        (1) To identify a study for which you want to conduct a replication. Especially recommended for studies that had unexpected findings.
        (2) To conduct a modified replication of a published study based on previous limitations such as a poor sampling.
            • A good possibility for a research topic is to plan a modified replication that overcomes one or more of the limitations discussed by a researcher in their own study.
        (3) To conduct a modified replication of a published study based on the researcher's insights after completing the study.
            • Researchers often briefly describe future directions for research in light of the insights they have gained from their study.

      c) A student researcher usually will find it helpful to be able to say that the proposed research will overcome the limitations of previous research or that the proposed research was suggested in a journal article for future research.

VIII. Using Demographics to Narrow a Topic

      a) If a topic seems too broad (e.g., patients' compliance with physicians' directions), it can often be made narrower by using one or more demographic characteristics such as studying only compliance by individuals with diabetes.

IX. Using Demographics to Make a Topic More Complex

      a) A research topic can also be made more complex by including one or more demographic variables.

X. Staying Open to Other Topics

      a) Do not settle on a topic before doing preliminary readings of the literature.

      b) Reading the literature might reveal that a number of studies have already been conducted on a given topic or that there is a consensus on the results among researchers.

      c) Sometimes a topic that seemed uninteresting has more interesting literature or has more important implications than anticipated.

Chapter 2: Locating Literature and Refining a Research Topic

I. Identifying Appropriate Databases
    a) Almost all journal articles are indexed in one or more electronic database.
    b) Identifying databases likely to have research on tentative research topics is key.
    c) ERIC (www.eric.ed.gov) stands for Education Resources Information Center.
        (1) Contains references to more than a million records that provide citations to journal articles, books, conference papers, and so on.
    d) PsycARTICLES and PsycINFO
        (1) Maintained by the American Psychological Association (APA).
        (2) PsycARTICLES contains more than 158,000 searchable *full-text articles* from 42 journals published by the APA and its allied organizations.
        (3) PsycINFO contains *abstracts* of more than 3.2 million references to both APA and non-APA journal articles and books.
    e) CSA Sociological Abstracts
        (1) Published by Cambridge Scientific Abstracts (CSA)—indexes abstracts of articles published in more than 250 English-language journals.
        (2) It abstracts dissertations, books, and unpublished papers.
        (3) This database also covers fields related to sociology including anthropology, criminology, social psychology, and urban studies.
    f) Social Work Abstracts
        (1) It indexes abstracts of articles in more than 460 social work and human services journals.
        (2) Also covers fields such as child and family welfare, civil rights, family welfare, drug and alcohol addiction, and various human services.
    g) Google Scholar (www.scholar.Google.com)
        (1) Searches scholarly literature across numerous disciplines.
        (2) Covers resources such as books, abstracts, and journal articles published by universities, professional societies, and academic publishers.
    h) Other databases such as Linguistics and Language Behavior Abstracts, Medline, Business Source Plus, and other specialized databases that may be accessed through an academic library. Consult a librarian for more information.
II. Using a Citation Index
    a) Google Scholar has a "Cited by" feature that indicates how many times the document has been cited and where.
    b) Information on citations can be important because a document that has been cited by other authors has probably been influential, controversial, or especially useful.
III. Using a Database Thesaurus
    a) If a database has a thesaurus of keywords on which it is structured, search the thesaurus for relevant terms (sometimes called *descriptors*).
IV. Using Boolean Operators (NOT, AND, and OR) to Refine a Search
    a) Using operators such as NOT as well as AND narrows the number of references found while using OR broadens the number.
    b) Boolean operators can also be used to delimit a search to selected demographics.
V. Searching for Theoretical Literature
    a) Because the development of theories is a major activity in the sciences, it is desirable to discuss relevant theories in literature reviews on most topics.
    b) Theoretical literature can be found by searching for a topic term then adding the term AND *theory.*
    c) Entering the name of a theory as a search term may yield references on that theory.

VI. Searching in Only the Title and/or Abstract Fields
    a) The information in databases is divided into fields, such as the author field, which allows users to search for articles written by a particular author.
    b) Two especially helpful fields:
        (1) Title field (the title of the work).
        (2) Abstract field (a summary of the work).

VII. Searching for the Works of a Particular Author
    a) Many researchers conduct research on a selected topic over a period of decades.
    b) To locate literature authored by such a researcher (and trace the history of that author's work on the topic), restrict a search to the author field.

VIII. Locating Statistics at www.FedStats.gov
    a) You can access statistics from more than 100 federal agencies.
    b) The Fed Stats site searches all agencies for relevant links to federal statistics.
    c) This is important for two reasons:
        (1) You do not have to search each agency separately.
        (2) An agency you are not aware of may have statistics relevant to a topic.
    d) Citing specific, relevant statistics when writing a literature review makes it more authoritative and informative.

IX. Keeping a Record of How the Search Was Conducted
    a) By being able to state specifically which databases were searched and how they were searched, reviewers can protect themselves from criticism that he or she was careless in conducting research.
    b) This is especially useful if a professor or researcher who is familiar with relevant experimental studies that a reviewer failed to locate challenges a statement made in a review.

X. Using a Coding System While Reading Literature
    a) An effective way to code is to use different colored highlighters.
    b) For example:
        (1) One color can be used for anything that is interesting or surprising.
        (2) Another can be used for discussions of relevant theories.
        (3) Another can be used for definitions of key terms.
        (4) And yet another can be used for suggestions for future research.

XI. Considering Literature When Selecting and Refining Topics
    a) Having located and considered the literature on several tentative topics, a researcher should be in a good position to make a selection among the topics.
    b) There are many ways in which the literature can assist in topic selection.
        (1) Results reported in literature on one topic might be more interesting than those on the others.
        (2) One topic might be less researched than the others.
        (3) One topic might have more practical implications than the others.
    c) Once one research topic has been selected over the others in a tentative list, consider how the literature might be used to refine the topic.
        (1) What demographics have been taken into account in previous research?
        (2) What limitations do previous researchers describe in their studies?
        (3) What do previous researchers suggest for future research?
    d) These considerations can often help identify how a topic can be refined or modified to make it more likely to contribute to the understanding of a topic.

Chapter 3: Preparing a Literature Review

I. Preparing a Table That Shows the Key Features of Each Article
    a) It is easy to get lost in details of individual articles and fail to see important trends and outcomes when there are several articles on in a topic.
    b) Preparing a table showing key features of each article can avoid this problem:
        (1) Give each article a unique identifier.
- A good identifier is the last name of the author and the year of publication.
- These should be listed in the first column of the table.

        (2) Contents of the remaining columns may vary substantially, depending on the literature to be reviewed. Some examples to consider are:
- Type of sample.
- Number of participants in the sample.
- Measurement approach.
- Overall results.
- Notable features.

        (3) Inspection of a table can aid in the further refinement of the research topic and reveal weaknesses to be avoided in one's own research.

II. Writing an Essay About the Literature
    a) A literature review is an essay that synthesizes information about a topic.
    b) The first step in writing such an essay is to prepare a topic outline.
        (1) Include the articles' identifiers, authors' last names and years of publication.
        (2) Note that a particular article might be cited at various points in the outline and that more than one article might be cited to support a particular point.
    c) Following a topic outline when writing a literature review will help prevent the common mistake of writing a string of summaries of one study after another.

III. Naming a Specific Topic Near the Beginning of a Review
    a) Do not start a review with broad, sweeping statements.
    b) Be specific and on point.

IV. Using Statistics to Establish the Importance of the Topic Near the Beginning of a Review
    a) Researchers frequently cite statistics near the beginning of a review to help indicate the importance of a problem.

V. Providing Conceptual Definitions Near the Beginning of a Review
    a) Providing conceptual definitions is especially important when related concepts might be confused with the topic of the research and ensures that terms are not mistakenly taken to mean something they are not intended to mean.

VI. Providing a Brief History of the Topic Near the Beginning of a Review
    a) Providing a brief history of the research on a topic can help establish the context for the proposed study.

VII. Writing a *Critical* Literature Review
    a) Uncritical reviews treat all studies as though they are equal in quality.
        (1) This can do a disservice to the reader, especially when there are contradictions in the literature.
    b) It is not always necessary to indicate the quality of studies cited, but in the absence of such indications readers are likely to assume the studies cited are of reasonable quality.
        (1) It is important to indicate that a weak study is being cited.
        (2) How much emphasis to put on the flaws of an individual study is ultimately a subjective decision.
        (3) Some indicators should be provided to warn readers when a study is seriously flawed by a weak sample or by serious design flaws, such as:
- Citing a study as a pilot or preliminary study.

- **Emphasizing** flaws by bolding the text.
  - (4) Sometimes it is more efficient to critique groups of studies that have common flaws.
  - c) An alternative to describing specific methodological weaknesses in studies is to use statements that indicate the degree of confidence that should be placed in them.
- VIII. Indicating the Level of Confidence in a Research Finding
  - a) All empirical research may safely be assumed to be subject to error.
  - b) As a result, it is important to use wording that does not imply that the research has revealed some universal fact or truth
  - c) Wording should be used to indicate the level of confidence the writer has in the results.
    - (1) Use statements to indicate a high level of confidence, such as:
      - "Overwhelming evidence"
      - "Strong evidence"
      - "Results of a definitive study"
      - "Seldom disputed"
      - "Seems very likely that"
    - (2) Use statements to indicate a low degree of confidence in the results of studies that are questionable, such as:
      - "Based on a pilot study"
      - "Weak evidence hints at"
      - "It appears that"
      - "Suggests the possibility that"
    - (3) It is not always necessary to use terms to indicate the degree of confidence. However, when the degree is not indicated, readers are likely to assume that the evidence is reasonably strong.
- IX. Pointing Out Consistent Findings in the Literature
  - a) There are subtle ways to point out findings that are consistent.
    - (1) For consistent results a phrase such as "it is commonly found," or "a great deal of support," can imply confidence in findings.
    - (2) For less consistent results phrasing such as "results tend to," implies a lesser degree of confidence.
- X. Pointing Out Gaps in the Literature
  - a) There are also subtle ways to point out findings that are inconsistent.
    - (1) For less consistent results, phrasing such as "results tend to," or "results fill a gap in the literature" implies a lesser degree of confidence.
- XI. Using Subheadings in a Long Review
  - a) Subheadings help readers to follow the transitions from one subtopic to another within a review.
  - b) The major subheadings in the topic outline usually serve as effective subheadings in a long review.
- XII. Describing Relevant Theories
  - a) It is very desirable to select a topic with theoretical underpinnings.
  - b) If you select such a topic, be sure to discuss the theory and its relationship to the topic in enough detail that a reader with no knowledge of the theory will be able to understand its importance.
  - c) Be sure to discuss relevant research that supports or contradicts the theory.
- XIII. Noting the Relationship Between the Review and the Research Questions, Purposes, or Hypotheses
  - a) A reader should see the logical connection between what is known about a topic and the research questions, purposes, or hypotheses underlying the research that will be conducted in a review.
  - b) Research questions, purposes, or hypotheses are usually near the end of a review.

Chapter 4: Citing References in APA and ASA Styles

I.   In-Text Citations
    a)   Citations identify the source of ideas and quotations used by a writer.
    b)   Typically, citations consist of two parts:
        (1) A symbol, such as an asterisk, letter of the alphabet, word, or number in the text.
        (2) A full bibliographic reference usually at the end of the material.
    c)   In-Text Citations in APA
        (1) American Psychological Association (APA) style uses a version of the "author–date" method for in-text citations and can be parenthetical or non-parenthetical.
        (2) Parenthetical In-Text Citations in APA Style
- An in-text citation can be made parenthetical by putting the author's name and year of publication in parentheses at the end of a quotation, paraphrase, or summary.
- For sources with two authors use an ampersand (&) between the last names of the authors. Example: (Smith, A. S. & Doe, F., 2013).
- When three to five authors of a given source are cited, the first time the authors are cited, all names are used.
- Then, in subsequent citations, only the first author's name followed by *et al.* is used. Example: (Smith, Doe & Jones, 2013) cited all subsequent times as (Smith et al., 2013)
- When a source being cited has six or more authors, use *et al.* every time it is cited.
- When two or more sources are in substantial agreement, multiple sources may be cited within a single set of parentheses in alphabetical order, separated by semicolons. Example: (Doe, 2013; Jones & Miller, 2012; Smith et al., 2013)
- When the source is a group, cite its authorship using the whole name of the group. Example: (Association for Hypothetical Studies, 2010)
- When an author wants to call attention to a specific passage within a source and quotes directly from a source, include the page number(s) in the in-text citation. Example: (Smith et al., 2013, pp. 6–7)
- *p.* serves as an abbreviation for page (singular) and *pp.* is the abbreviation for pages.
        (3) Non-Parenthetical In-Text Citations in APA Style
- An in-text citation can be non-parenthetical as well.
- For non-parenthetical in-text citations, the author's last name is used as the subject of the sentence, while the year of publication remains parenthetical.
- The word *and* is used instead of an ampersand (&) for non-parenthetical in-text citations.
- Non-parenthetical in-text citations are best used when a writer wants to emphasize the authorship of the source material.
        (4) Reference Lists in APA Style
- For each in-text citation there should be a full bibliographic reference in the reference list at the end of the manuscript.
- References in a reference list are formatted with second and subsequent lines indented with a "hanging indent."
- Print and electronic references should be combined into a single list with the heading "References," which should be centered and in bold.
- Consult the *APA Style Guide* for more information on how to format different types of references.

      d) In-Text Citations in ASA Style
- (1) ASA stands for the American Sociological Society. Like APA style, ASA style uses a version of the "author–date" method for in-text citations. This method can also be parenthetical or non-parenthetical.
- (2) Parenthetical In-Text Citations in ASA Style
  - Much like in APA. An in-text citation in ASA style can be made parenthetical by putting the author's last name and year of publication in parentheses. Unlike APA, a comma does not separate the last name and date. Example: (Doe 2013)
  - For sources written by two authors the word *and* is used. Example: (Smith and Doe 2013)
  - Sources with one or two authors cited more than once in a given manuscript should be cited the same way each time.
  - When there are three authors of a given source, the first time the authors are cited, all names are used. In subsequent citations, only the first author's name followed by *et al.* is used. Example: (Smith, Doe, and Jones 2013) cited all subsequent times as (Smith et al. 2013)
  - When a source has four or more authors use *et al.* the first and all subsequent times. Example: (Smith et al. 2013)
  - If two or more sources are in substantial agreement the sources may be cited within a single set of parentheses. Like APA Style the sources are listed in alphabetical order separated by semicolons. Example: (Doe 2013; Jones and Miller 2012; Smith et al. 2013)
  - When the source is a group, cite its authorship using the sole name of the group. Example: (Association for Hypothetical Studies 2010)
  - To call attention to a specific passage within a source quoted directly from the source, include the page number(s) in the in-text citation. Example: (Jones et al. 2013: 6-7)
- (3) Non-parenthetical in-text citations are done the same way in both APA and ASA style, with the author's last name as the subject of the sentence and the year of publication remaining parenthetical.
- (4) In ASA Style and APA Style, each reference is formatted with a hanging indent.

II. Reference Management Software
      a) For those who are undertaking large research projects and will need help managing and organizing many references, there is a variety of reference management software available, ranging in price from free to hundreds of dollars.
      b) Reference management software offers a variety of features for researchers, including the ability to:
- (1) Bookmark web pages.
- (2) Tag, annotate, and highlight PDFs.
- (3) Create a reference list based on hundreds of different reference styles.

      c) Some software is only available through the web, while some may be downloaded directly to your computer.
      d) Students may sign up for accounts through their university to access the software for free.

III. Concluding Comments
      a) APA style and ASA style differ primarily in details regarding punctuation and placement of various types of information.
      b) They may just be details, but they are important details in scientific writing, where consistency in style is important in order to avoid misunderstandings and errors.

Chapter 5: Writing Research Hypotheses, Purposes, and Questions

I. Writing Research Hypotheses
  a) A research hypothesis predicts the outcome of a research study.
    (1) The prediction may be based on theory, results of previous research, or a combination of both.
  b) Hypotheses are usually stated near the end of a literature review.
  c) To be an effective guide for research, a hypothesis should refer to specific variables.
  d) Some hypotheses refer to treatments that will be administered to participants.
  e) Under most circumstances, a hypothesis should *not* refer to a specific statistical outcome, because if the outcome is off by even 1% the researcher will have to report that the hypothesis was not confirmed.
  f) A hypothesis should *not* state a value judgment because such judgments are not observable.
  g) If there are a number of hypotheses to be investigated in a study, consider presenting them in a numbered list.
    (1) This will make it easier to write the results section of the research report by permitting reference to the hypotheses by number.
II. Writing Research Purposes
  a) If a researcher wants to explore a particular topic but believes they are unable to predict the results, a research purpose should be stated in lieu of a research hypothesis.
  b) Like a hypothesis, a research purpose should refer to specific observable behaviors.
III. Writing Research Questions
  a) A research question serves as an alternative to writing a research purpose.
  b) When the question form is used, it should be stated in a way that it cannot be answered with a simple "yes" or "no" because the results of research are usually mixed.
    (1) Normally, there will be *some degree* of social influence, which could not be described accurately with a simple "yes" or "no."
IV. Identifying Populations in Research Hypotheses, Purposes, and Questions
  a) When a researcher is interested in studying how variables operate in specific types of populations, the populations should be identified within the research hypothesis, purpose, or question.
    (1) This ensures that the reader will have the same context as the author with which to view the research.
V. Referring to Measurement Methods in Research Hypotheses, Purposes, and Questions
  a) Not necessary to name specific measures in research hypotheses, purposes, or questions.
    (1) These measures can be discussed in detail later in a research proposal or report.
    (2) Main exception to this guideline is when a specific measure is the subject of the research.
VI. Concluding Comments
  a) Consider writing several research hypotheses, purposes, or questions and asking for feedback on them from instructors and other students.
  b) Having several to compare and contrast will facilitate a discussion of each as the basis for a research project.

Chapter 6: Selecting a Research Approach

I. Experimental Versus Nonexperimental Research
   a) The purpose of experimentation is to explore a cause-and-effect relationship.
   b) All experiments have at least one independent and one dependent variable.
      (1) The independent variable, such as providing daily versus weekly feedback, constitutes the variable that is under the control of the experimenter.
      (2) The outcome variable, out of the experimenter's control, is called the dependent variable.
   c) A classic design for an experiment is to form an experimental group that receives a new or alternative treatment and a control group that receives either no treatment or a conventional treatment.
   d) Often, researchers want to explore causality but cannot administer the treatments of interest for practical reasons or for legal or ethical reasons. In cases such as these, the best option is to find participants who have received such treatments previously.
      (1) Note that such a study is nonexperimental because no treatments were administered for the study. Instead, it is a type of nonexperimental study known as a causal-comparative study.

II. Major Types of Nonexperimental Research
   a) Causal-Comparative Research
      (1) Nonexperimental research can be used to explore causality but only when it is not possible to conduct an experiment by administering treatments to participants.
      (2) The primary type of quantitative nonexperimental research for exploring causality is *causal-comparative research* (*ex post facto research*).
      (3) A researcher should choose the causal-comparative method if three conditions are met:
         • The goal is to investigate a cause-and-effect relationship.
         • Treatments cannot be given.
         • Two similar groups that differ in some outcome can be identified and questioned.
   b) Surveys
      (1) Surveys provide what currently exists, not what caused its existence.
      (2) Questionnaires are the most popular method for collecting survey information.
         • Questionnaires sent through the mail have a very low response rate.
      (3) Face-to-face interviews are also widely used in surveys.
         • The interview process has numerous advantages.
      (4) For educational research, achievement surveys are also popular.
   c) Correlational Studies
      (1) A correlational study is designed to examine the relationship between two or more sets of scores—the term correlational research is almost always reserved as a label for studies in which correlation coefficient is employed.
         • It can be computed only when there are two sets of scores.
      (2) A correlation coefficient can vary from 0.00 to 1.00 for direct relationships. A value of 0.00 indicates the complete absence of a relationship while a 1.00 indicates a perfect direct relationship.
      (3) A correlation coefficient can also vary from 0.00 to -1.00 for inverse relationships. A value of 0.00 indicates the complete absence of a relationship while a -1.00 indicates a perfect inverse relationship.
   d) Document/Content-Analysis Research
      (1) Human behavior is at times explored by examining the contents of documents.
         • An advantage of document/content-analysis research is that good

samples can often be obtained.

- A disadvantage of document/content-analysis research is that an assumption must be made that the contents of documents accurately reflect the attitudes and beliefs of those who wrote them and those who read them.

(2) While document/content-analysis research can provide informative results, conducting such research is greatly simplified by not having to deal directly with research participants.

III. Program Evaluation: A Hybrid

a) The evaluation of social and educational programs has become a major focus of researchers since the 1960s.

b) Program evaluation is a "hybrid" because some evaluation efforts have similarities to experimental research while others have similarities to nonexperimental research.

c) The programs that are administered can be viewed as treatments given to participants.

(1) Unlike researchers who conduct experiments, program evaluators seldom have control over the decision on who will receive the treatment and who will not.

d) Some elements of program evaluation do not deal with the effects or outcomes of the programs. Instead, they deal with factors affecting their implementation.

IV. Quantitative Versus Qualitative Research

a) A major distinction in research is whether it is quantitative or qualitative.

(1) In quantitative research, the results are reduced to numbers, typically scores or frequency counts that can be analyzed with statistical methods.

- In order to make such an analysis meaningful, procedures used to obtain the scores must be standardized so that they are the same for each participant.

i. Quantitative studies should be carefully and fully planned in advance to enhance the collection of data in a standardized way.

ii. Once a quantitative study is started, deviations from the plans should not be permitted because they may interfere with the standardization.

iii. Personalized interactions with participants should not be permitted because these might disrupt the standardization, causing different kinds of interactions with different participants.

- Quantitative research might be characterized as being rigid, distant, and impersonal.

(2) In qualitative research, there is no need to standardize the data collection. It does not need to be as fully planned in advance, and deviations in the plans cannot only be tolerated but might be welcomed.

(3) For example, semi-structured interviews might be used to gather qualitative data and interviewers might be encouraged to probe in different directions with different participants.

b) Put in general terms, quantitative researchers have the potential for more breadth in understanding a problem and qualitative researchers have the potential for more depth of understanding.

c) While it might be argued that a researcher should pick a topic and then use the most appropriate methods (whether quantitative or qualitative) to study it, in reality, some researchers are more comfortable working with quantities while others are more skilled in working with a less structured approach.

(1) Those with a strong orientation should consider it when selecting a topic because some topics naturally lend themselves more to a quantitative approach while others lend themselves more to a qualitative approach.

Chapter 7: Looking Ahead to Participant Selection

I. Determining the Number of Participants to Use
  a) There is no answer to determine how many participants are needed for a study. It depends on a number of factors:
    (1) If the research is being conducted for a term project, small numbers of participants might be acceptable, depending on the requirements.
    (2) For a thesis or dissertation, numbers larger than those required for a term project probably will be expected and, once again, the advice of instructors is needed to make a final determination of the appropriate sample size.
    (3) There are varying norms for different types of research.
    (4) Some types of participants are difficult to locate or work with as participants.
  b) How the participants are selected is much more important than how many are selected.
  c) Examining the literature is one of the most fruitful ways to identify norms for the numbers of participants used in various types of studies on various topics.
    (1) Being able to cite the number of participants used in previous studies can be an important strength when justifying plans for a particular number of participants in a term project, thesis, or dissertation.
II. Random Sampling for Quantitative Research
  a) Random sampling is the gold standard for selecting a sample from a population.
    (1) In this type of sampling, all members of a population must be identified, and each member must be given an equal chance of being selected.
  b) Random sampling is sometimes not used because even though it is desirable, it is frequently difficult to identify all members of a population.
  c) Another common reason random sampling is sometimes not used is because some potential participants whose names are selected by random sampling may refuse to participate.
    (1) Even if a random sample of names is drawn, the refusal of some of those selected to participate makes the actual resulting sample nonrandom and therefore biased.
III. Stratified Sampling for Quantitative Research
  a) In stratified sampling, a sample that is representative of its population in terms of key variables is drawn.
  b) In stratified random sampling, the same percentage of individuals is drawn at random from each subgroup.
  c) Stratification is not always conducted with random sampling, but using stratification without random sampling is not as useful as it might seem.
IV. Convenience Sampling for Quantitative and Qualitative Research
  a) The use of volunteers serves as an example of convenience sampling.
  b) Convenience samples must be presumed to be biased samples; however, they still have a legitimate role in both quantitative and qualitative research.
    (1) They allow researchers who do not have access to better samples an opportunity to make preliminary explorations related to their research hypotheses, purposes, or questions.
    (2) They allow researchers to pilot test their measurement techniques.
    (3) Promising research with convenience samples may inspire researchers with access to better samples to replicate the research.
V. Purposive Sampling for Qualitative Research
  a) Qualitative researchers tend to emphasize depth of understanding of purposively selected, small groups of individuals without regard to the appropriateness of generalizing from them to a population.
  b) In purposive sampling, individuals are handpicked to be participants because they have certain characteristics that are believed to make them especially good sources of

information.

    c)   The distinction between a purposive sample and a sample of convenience is important because selecting a purposive sample is regarded as highly appropriate for a qualitative study, while using a sample of convenience should be avoided whenever possible in both qualitative and quantitative research.

    d)   To qualify as a purposive sample a researcher must:

        (1) Establish criteria for the selection of certain types of individuals.

        (2) Have a reason for establishing the criteria.

        (3) Make a planned and systematic effort to contact such individuals.

    e)   If a sample of convenience is the only available option, a study should not necessarily be abandoned. Conducting the research in spite of this weakness in sampling has some benefit:

        (1) It allows beginning researchers to gain experience that will be useful in later projects.

        (2) A pilot qualitative study with a sample of convenience will help to determine whether additional research with a better sample is likely to be fruitful.

VI. Using Literature When Making Plans for Participant Selection

    a)   Beginning researchers who will be conducting research as a term project should make some preliminary plans based on the information in this chapter and the descriptions of participant selection found in the literature on their topic—note how many participants were used in various studies as well as how they were selected.

    b)   Often, authors of published research discuss limitations in participant selection in the "Discussion" section near the end of research reports.

Chapter 8: Looking Ahead to Measurement

I. Using Measures Employed in Previous Research
    a) When investigating a topic, researchers often use the same measures previously employed by other researchers who investigated the topic.
    b) Using the same measures has two potential advantages:
        (1) Much is often known about the validity of measures used in previous research, especially if they have been widely used.
            • The frequency of prior use suggests that other researchers have judged the measure to be valid.
        (2) It helps in building a consistent body of research.
    c) Research problems may require a modification of measures used in previous research.
    d) A disadvantage of using a measure widely used in previous studies on a topic is that whatever flaws the measure has will affect the results of all the studies.
        (1) There may be times where a justification for conducting another study on the same topic is to determine if similar results can be obtained using a different measure or even a different type of measure.

II. Locating Existing Measures
    a) Reviewing the literature on a topic frequently identifies existing measures.
        (1) When researchers have difficulty in locating a particular measure, they can consult the Educational Testing Service's (ETS) Test Collection Database.
            • This database contains descriptions of more than 25,000 measures, including research and unpublished measures.
            • For each measure, the database includes information on the availability such as the name, address, and phone number of the author or publisher.
    b) The ETS Test Collection Database is useful for locating measures on specialized topics.

III. Issues in Devising New Measures
    a) Sometimes, new measures need to be devised to suit a particular research project.
        (1) The general rule is that if a match between the research goal and the measures can be improved greatly by devising a new measure, a new one should be devised.
    b) Beginning researchers should note that when they devise new measures, they might be asked to defend the measures' validity and reliability (in quantitative research) or dependability and credibility (in qualitative research).

IV. Validity of Measures in Quantitative Research
    a) In quantitative research, the validity of measures is of great concern.
        (1) Validity refers to the extent to which the measures are measuring what they are supposed to be measuring.
    b) One of the major approaches to studying the validity of measures is to conduct statistical studies in which the results from administering a measure are correlated with other results.
    c) The other major approach to studying validity is to have experts make judgments regarding the contents of a measure.
    d) Be aware that the validity of measures should be addressed in a research report, so attention should be paid to any available validity information on measures being considered for use in a research project.

V. Reliability of Measures in Quantitative Research

      a) Reliability deals with the extent to which results are consistent.

      b) Consistency in measurement is desirable whenever a relatively stable trait is being measured.

      c) One of the most important factors influencing the reliability of objective tests and scales is the number of items they contain.

          (1) Reliability is an especially important concern when the measure requires subjective judgments because these judgments can be quite unreliable if they are highly subjective.

          (2) For this reason, quantitative researchers prefer measures that de-emphasize subjectivity.

VI. Credibility of Measures in Qualitative Research

      a) The credibility of the measure in qualitative research is roughly equivalent to the concept of validity of measure in quantitative research. Except, different approaches are used to obtain it:

          (1) *Member checks* is a method that consists of sharing the interpretations of results with participants to gauge how well the interpretations reflect the meanings intended by participants.

          (2) Prolonged engagement in the field is also a method used for assuring credibility.

          (3) When resources do not permit prolonged engagement, time sampling can enhance credibility.

      b) Qualitative researchers also use what they call "triangulation of data sources," which means using more than one type of source for data.

      c) Students who are planning qualitative research should make some preliminary decisions on what steps they might take to enhance the credibility of their measures.

VII. Dependability of Measures in Qualitative Research

      a) Qualitative researchers are more tolerant of subjectivity in their measures than quantitative researchers, but they do concern themselves with whether their subjectivity is sufficiently controlled so that the results reflect on the participants without undue influence of those making the subjective judgments.

      b) One way to examine dependability in qualitative research is to have more than one individual code and interpret the data (such as the responses to open-ended questions) and note the extent to which they both agree.

          (1) When areas of disagreement among the individuals emerge, they can be resolved through discussions designed to lead to a consensus on the best interpretations.

          (2) A consensus is usually taken to be more dependable than a single individual's judgment.

      c) Dependability in qualitative research can also be improved through the use of "triangulation of measure."

          (1) Unlike triangulation of data sources, in which various types of sources are employed, triangulation of measure uses only one source but uses more than one type of measure.

          (2) To the extent that different types of measures yield similar results, the results can be said to be dependable.

Chapter 9: Looking Ahead to Data Analysis for Quantitative Research

I. Analysis of Nominal Data
   a) Many variables in research yield what is called *nominal data.*
      (1) Nominal data use words instead of numbers to describe their categories.
   b) Percentages
      (1) Percentages are widely used to analyze nominal data.
         • A percentage indicates the number of cases per 100 that have some characteristic.
      (2) *Contingency tables* are used when researchers are interested in the relationship between two nominal variables. These two-way tables can help in determining whether a relationship exists.
         • It is important to indicate the number of cases in a contingency table because percentages, by themselves, can sometimes be misleading.
   c) Chi-Square
      (1) The possibility that random samples differ from each other only because of random sampling is called the *null hypothesis.* Two equally acceptable ways of expressing this hypothesis are:
         • Random sampling has created a difference between the samples that does not exist between populations.
         • There is no true difference between the populations.
      (2) The relationship between two nominal variables, the null hypothesis can be tested using a chi-square test.
         • A chi-square test aids in finding whether or not a relationship is statistically significant.
II. Analysis of Group Differences in Interval Variables
   a) In contrast to nominal variables, an *interval variable* has numbers that represent how much of something exists.
   b) Tests and scales that have objective-type items that yield overall scores often generate interval data in the social and behavioral sciences.
   c) Means and Standard Deviations for One Group
      (1) The central tendency for interval data can be described with an average. In statistics, there are three averages:
         • Mean
         • Median
         • Mode
      (2) By far, the mean is the most widely used. It is the average that is obtained by summing all the scores and dividing by the number of scores.
      (3) While knowing the average of a set of scores is very informative, an average does not indicate how spread out the scores are.
         • The technical term for the "amount of spread" in a set of scores is variability.
      (4) One way to describe variability is to report the range of scores, as in "the scores range from 2 to 80."
      (5) However, a much more common way to describe variability is to use the *standard deviation*, which was designed to indicate the variability of the middle two thirds of a group.
         • For example:
   d) Means and Standard Deviations for Two or More Groups
      (1) While the analysis of the means and standard deviations for two or more groups is much the same, the distinction comes in how it is reported.

- Be careful to report information for different groups separately to keep the results clear.

e) *t* Test for Two Means

    (1) To test the null hypothesis between two means, a test called the *t* test can be used.

    (2) A value of *t* can be computed and used to determine the probability that the null hypothesis is true. As with the chi-square test, if the probability is .05 or less (such as .01 or .001), the null hypothesis should be rejected.

f) Analysis of Variance (ANOVA) for More Than Two Means

    (1) Because the *t* test is used for comparing only two means, its use is not appropriate for a purpose that will generate interval data for more than two groups.

    (2) For more than two means, *analysis of variance* (ANOVA) can be used.

    (3) Once again, if the entire population of the groups is tested, there is no need to test the null hypothesis because it refers to sampling errors, which do not exist when there is no sampling.

III. Analysis of Change on Interval Variables

a) Researchers administer pretests and posttests in order to measure the amount of change.

b) A classic model is a two-group experiment in which an experimental group receives a pretest, followed by a treatment, followed by a posttest. In the meantime, a control group receives a pretest, followed by no special treatment, followed by a posttest.

    (1) By subtracting each participant's posttest score from his or her pretest score, a change score is obtained.

    (2) The usual analysis for such a setup is to calculate the means and standard deviations for the pretest, posttest, and change scores for each group.

IV. Analysis for the Relationship Between Two Interval Variables

a) When examining the relationship between two interval variables, the most widely used statistic is the correlation coefficient (informally called the *Pearson r*).

    (1) A correlation coefficient describes the direction of a relationship. The direction of a relationship is either direct (also called positive) or inverse (also called negative).

- Note that coefficients for a direct relationship range from 0.00 to 1.00, with 0.00 indicating no relationship and 1.00 indicating a perfect direct relationship. For an inverse relationship, the range is from 0.00 (no relationship) to −1.00 for a perfect negative relationship.

b) When correlation coefficients are reported, it is conventional to also report the mean and standard deviation.

Chapter 10: Looking Ahead to Data Analysis for Qualitative Research

I.   The Intermingling of Data Collection and Data Analysis
   a)   Preliminary, informal data analysis is usually performed during the process of collecting the data in qualitative research.
   b)   This is illustrated by three practices commonly employed by qualitative researchers. While collecting data, qualitative researchers often engage in memo writing where the interviewers make notes of their own reactions and interpretations.
      (1)   As data are being collected, qualitative researchers reflect on it (a form of informal analysis) and use their reflections as a basis for modifying questions, formulating additional questions, and even changing the line of questioning in order to obtain more useful data.
      (2)   Qualitative researchers often collect data from additional participants until they reach the point of data saturation.
         • This refers to the failure of additional cases to add new information beyond what was collected from previous participants.

II. Selecting a General Approach to Data Analysis
   a)   To guide their data analysis, qualitative researchers usually select a general, overarching approach.
   b)   The Grounded Theory Approach
      (1)   Perhaps the most frequently used approach is the *grounded theory approach*.
      (2)   The term "theory" in "grounded theory" can be a bit misleading because it does not refer to a theory of human behavior. Instead, it refers to an inductive method of analysis that can lead to theories of behavior.
         • Qualitative researchers start with the data and develop theories based on the data (i.e., grounded in the data).
      (3)   First step—open coding. In this step, segments of the transcripts of the interviews are examined for distinct, separate segments (such as ideas or experiences of the participants) and are "coded" by identifying them and giving each type a name.
      (4)   Second step—axial coding. At this stage, the transcripts of the interviews and any other data sources, such as memos written during data collection, are reexamined with the purpose of identifying relationships between the categories and themes identified during open coding.
         • There are several types of relationships that might be noted. Here are a few examples:
            i.   Temporal [X usually precedes Y in linear time].
            ii. Causal [X caused participants to do Y].
            iii. Associational [X and Y usually or always occur at about the same time but are not believed to be causally connected].
      (5)   In the final stages of the grounded theory approach to analysis, qualitative researchers develop a *core category*, which is the main overarching category under which the other categories and subcategories belong.
   c)   Consensual Qualitative Approach
      (1)   Hill's *Consensual Qualitative Research* approach (CQR), which emphasizes having several individuals participate in the analysis, has specific steps designed to lead to a consensus regarding the meaning and interpretation of the results.
         • CQR specifies a series of procedures to code the data across participant responses.

III. Specific Techniques for Analysis of Qualitative Data
    a) Enumeration
        (1) Enumeration is counting how many respondents mentioned each important construct (such as a feeling, behavior, or incident).
        (2) By subtracting each participant's posttest score from his or her pretest score, a change score is obtained. The usual analysis for such a setup is to calculate the means and standard deviations for the pretest, posttest, and change scores for each group.
        (3) Some researchers use the results in writing up their results.
            • Using terms such as "many," "some," and "a few" based on enumeration data makes it possible to discuss the results without cluttering them with specific numbers and percentages
        (4) When correlation coefficients are reported, it is conventional to also report the mean and standard deviation.
    b) Selecting Quotations
        (1) It is very common to present quotations from participants to illustrate points made in the results section of a qualitative research report.
            • Preliminary decisions should be made on which quotations to use during data analysis.
        (2) Perhaps the most common criterion for the selection of quotations is that they are somehow "representative," which might be indicated by how frequently something is said.
        (3) Another criterion is the degree to which a quotation articulates main ideas in the results.
        (4) And yet another is intensity.
            • Statements made with strong words or higher-than-normal volume might indicate an emotional intensity associated with the statements.
    c) Intercoder Agreement
        (1) It is desirable to have two or more researchers code the data when possible.
            • It is customary to have them consult with each other to determine the general approach and the specific techniques that will be employed.
            • Then they begin working independently.
        (2) Later, the researchers consult with each other to determine the extent to which their codes and interpretations are in agreement. If the researchers largely agree, this is evidence of the dependability of the results. While large areas of disagreement indicate that the data are subject to more than one good interpretation.
        (3) The researchers might then work together to strive to reach a consensus on the results, which is an important feature of CQR.
    d) Diagramming
        (1) Having performed the analysis, qualitative researchers often diagram the results by placing the core concept in a box at the top and showing the array of related categories below it.
    e) Auditing
        (1) To use auditing, a researcher must keep detailed accounts of how the data were collected and the thought processes used while analyzing the data.
            • Some of these accounts might be in the form of memos.
        (2) Auditing is similar to peer debriefing in that a qualified outsider is used for the activity. However, in peer debriefing, the outsider acts more as a consultant who is assisting the researcher. In auditing, the auditor is more

like an outside financial auditor for a corporation.

     (3) The auditor's role is not to participate in the research but to examine it near the end in the hope that he or she will be able to certify the appropriateness of the research methods and interpretations of the results.

f) Member Checks

     (1) When conducting member checks, participants are asked to meet again with the researcher to review the data and results.

- For instance, they can be asked to verify the accuracy of the transcriptions of the interviews, and they can be asked to comment on the adequacy of the interpretations of the data.

     (2) When participants disagree with certain interpretations, the researcher should explore how they might be reformulated to take into account the participants' views.

     (3) Conducting thorough member checks can be quite time-consuming. As a consequence, qualitative researchers sometimes ask only a sample of the original participants to participate in this activity.

g) Identifying the Range of Responses

     (1) Even when all or almost all respondents provide similar accounts in terms of content, their responses can range in emotional tone as well as in frequency.

- Noting the range of responses when analyzing the data can assist in writing up the results.

h) Discrepant Case Analysis

     (1) During data analysis, it is important to note and consider discrepant cases.

     (2) Researchers should consider whether there are other ways that might explain the discrepancy in which the minority differs from the majority.

- If an answer is not clear, it might be useful to ask some of the discrepant cases to return for another interview.

Chapter 11: Preparing a Preliminary Research Proposal

I. The Title of a Proposal
    a) The title of a proposal should be a brief statement that names the major variables in the research hypothesis, purpose, or question.
        (1) It might also include types of individuals covered by the research.
    b) To distinguish a proposal from a report of completed research, researchers often give it this subtitle: "A Research Proposal."
    c) The title is not a sentence and does not end with a period.

II. The Introduction and Literature Review
    a) Student researchers should seek guidance on whether they are expected to begin their proposal with an introduction followed by a separate literature review *or* to begin with an essay that integrates the two elements.
        (1) If the introduction is to be a separate essay, it should contain the following elements:
- Identification of the problem area.
- Conceptual definitions of key terms.
- An indication of why the topic is worthy of investigation, including the types of implications the results might have.
- A brief description of any relevant theories, which should be expanded on in the literature review.
- A statement of the specific research hypotheses, purposes, or questions the research is designed to explore.

    b) A *conceptual definition* is a dictionary-like definition that sets the general boundaries that establish the meaning of a construct.
    c) Conversely, *operational definitions* describe the physical process used to identify the construct and "see" it.
        (1) While conceptual definitions are presented in the introduction to a research proposal, operational definitions typically are presented in the "Methods" section of a proposal.
    d) The Introduction and Literature Review in Qualitative Research
        (1) Qualitative researchers might recognize that their personal perspectives and experiences may influence their collection and interpretation of data in the introduction.
        (2) Proposals for qualitative research seldom contain hypotheses because qualitative researchers emphasize "following the data."

III. The Method Section of a Proposal
    a) The "Method" section is given the major heading "Method," which is usually centered on the page.
    b) It almost always has at least two subsections, one on participant selection and one on measures.
    c) Participants
        (1) Start this subsection with a description of the population from which the participants will be selected and state the basis for selection:
- e.g., random selection, convenience sampling, etc.
- If a sample of convenience (also known as an accidental sample) is used, it is a good idea to explicitly acknowledge this as a weakness.

        (2) Indicate how many names will be drawn.
        (3) Provide a best guess as to the rate of participation.
        (4) Describe the informed consent procedures used, if any.

(5) Discuss any anticipated limitations in the selection of participants and, if possible, discuss how these might affect the results.

d) Measures

(1) The measures subsection should describe the measures such as questionnaires, interview questions or tests that will be used in the research.

(2) Qualitative researchers frequently interview participants using semi-structured or loosely structured interviews.

(3) Even though they will not be highly structured, the "Measures" section of a proposal should indicate the types of information that will be collected with the interviews.

(4) Quantitative researchers usually use objective-type measures.

(5) If new measures will be developed, the description of them should be as specific as possible.

e) Procedures

(1) The optional subsection called "Procedures" is usually flush left in italics under the major heading of "Method."

• It usually follows the subsections on "Participants" and "Measures."

(2) The subsection on procedures is needed whenever there are important physical steps that will be taken in order to conduct the research that were not described under "Participants" and "Measures."

(3) A common use for the "Procedures" subsection is to describe the steps that will be taken to administer the measures.

• The proposed procedures for an experiment should also be described.

i. Sometimes this is presented under another subheading labeled "Experimental Procedures."

IV. The Analysis Section of a Proposal

a) The "Analysis" section is given the major heading "Analysis," which is usually centered on the page.

(1) For a quantitative proposal for basic research, this section can be rather brief, naming the statistics that will be computed.

(2) The "Analysis" section of a qualitative proposal may be somewhat longer than that of a quantitative proposal if the general approach is to be described in detail.

b) It is usually not considered necessary to indicate whether a statistical computer program will be used for a quantitative proposal.

c) However, if a computer program will be used in qualitative analysis, it should be named because the available programs differ greatly in their underlying assumptions and approaches to the more loosely structured data generated by qualitative studies.

V. The Discussion Section of a Proposal

a) The Discussion section is given the major heading "Discussion," which is usually centered on the page.

b) Typically, this section begins with a brief summary of the proposal up to that point.

(1) The summary should describe not only the mechanical aspects of the study, but also restate the research hypotheses, purposes, or questions to be explored as well as the context for the study.

c) A description of the limitations and strengths of the study should be included.

VI. References at the End of a Proposal

a) The "References" section is given the major heading "References," which is usually centered on the page.

(1) This section should include only references that were cited in the proposal. The references should not constitute "a suggested reading list."

VII.   The Major Components of a Proposal: An Outline

Title: The Influence of X on Y Among Residents of
King County: A Research Proposal

Introduction

Literature Review

Method

Participants

Measures

Procedures (or *Experimental Procedures*)

Analysis

Discussion

References

a) It is important to put the preliminary plans for research in writing as a preliminary research proposal early in the research process.
   (1) This will allow time for the writer to later review the proposal with a fresh mindset as well as to obtain feedback from others, which can be used in improving it.

Part B
Issues in Participant Selection

Chapter 12: Participant Selection in Quantitative Research

I. Simple Random Sampling
   a) The only way to preclude bias in sampling is to draw a *random sample* of names and to convince all those individuals whose names have been selected to participate in the study.
      (1) Conventional wisdom dictates that if a sample is not drawn at random, it should be presumed to be biased.
   b) *Simple random sampling* consists of giving each member of a population an equal and independent chance of being selected.
      (1) Conceptually, the simplest way to do this is to write the names of all members of a population on slips of paper, put them in a container, and draw the number needed for the sample.
         • With this process, each individual has a chance of being selected.
      (2) Another way to draw a simple random sample is to use a table of random numbers.
   c) It is important to note that because a sample is random (and therefore unbiased), it is not necessarily free of errors. In fact, it is safe to presume that all random samples have been influenced by random errors (i.e., chance errors).
      (1) A major advantage of random sampling is that a class of statistics known as inferential statistics allows researchers to estimate how likely it is that the results have been influenced by random sampling errors.

II. Stratified Random Sampling
   a) Random selection can be improved by combining it with stratification on a relevant variable. When a researcher stratifies, he or she divides the population into subgroups, each of which has a common characteristic.
      (1) Typically, a researcher will draw from each subgroup to reflect its demographic percentages. It is possible to stratify on more than one variable.

III. Systematic Sampling
   a) Sampling is drawing every *n*th individual from a list, where *n* is the interval size such as a small interval of 2 or a larger interval of 10.
   b) A potential weakness of systematic sampling is that the population list might be ordered in such a way that a biased sample is selected.
      (1) To avoid this type of problem, an alphabetical list should be used. Furthermore, selections should be made all the way through the list.
      (2) Even though systematic sampling is not random, using an alphabetical list and drawing throughout the list until the end of the list is reached is considered, for all practical purposes, to be as good as random sampling.

IV. Cluster Sampling
   a) *Cluster sampling* can be used when all members of a population are already assembled into groups.
      (1) Each group is called a cluster, and clusters instead of individuals are selected for a sample.
   b) An advantage of cluster sampling is that it is often more convenient to draw clusters instead of individuals.
   c) For cluster sampling to qualify as an excellent method of sampling, two conditions must be met and a reasonable number of clusters must be drawn, regardless of the number of individuals in them. The clusters must be drawn at random.

V. Sample Size in Quantitative Research

a) There is no easy answer to the question of what size a sample should be.
b) Five examples were given in a previous chapter:
    (1) The requirements of an instructor regarding sample size for a term project.
    (2) The requirements for a thesis or dissertation.
    (3) The norms for different types of research, which can often be determined by noting the sample sizes in publishing research of various types.
    (4) The difficulty of locating some types of participants.
    (5) Trading off a smaller sample in favor of obtaining a more diverse sample.
c) Potential for Harm to Participants
    (1) If it is anticipated that potential harm might result from procedures used in a research study, then initial studies using very small numbers of participants should be conducted.
        • This will allow researchers to determine the possible magnitude of the harm as well as the benefits.
d) The Need for Pilot Studies
    (1) A pilot study is an initial study that is conducted to determine feasibility. Pilot studies can contribute to knowledge on a topic and often are publishable in an academic journal when their results are especially promising and the rationale underlying the research is demanding.
e) Number of Subgroups to be Examined
    (1) As a general rule, the more subgroups that will be examined in a study, the larger the total sample size should be.
f) Importance of Precise Results
    (1) The larger the sample, the more precise the results are.
    (2) If highly precise results are needed, then very large samples should be used.
g) Statistical Significance
    (1) A statistically significant difference is one that is larger than one would expect on the basis of chance alone.
    (2) One of the key factors in significance testing is sample size. The larger the sample, the more likely a given difference is statistically significant.

Chapter 13: Participant Selection in Qualitative Research

I. Purposive Sampling
   a) Criterion Sampling
      (1) Used when very clear-cut, specific criteria are established for identifying potential participants.
      (2) When planning participant selection, consider exclusion criteria as well as inclusion criteria.
   b) Random Purposive Sampling
      (1) When the potential purposive sample is too large, random selection within the purposive sample can help decrease the sample.
   c) Typical Case Sampling
      (1) Sometimes beneficial to select participants who are "typical" or "normal" in some sense.
      (2) Advantage: reduces the complexity of the data collected, making analysis easier.
      (3) Disadvantage: Sometimes comparing typical cases with extreme/deviant cases can reveal too much.
   d) Extreme or Deviant Sampling
      (1) Criteria should be established to identify what constitutes an "extreme/deviant" case in a particular study.
      (2) Individuals who meet the criteria should be purposively selected.
      (3) Can be useful to conduct initial study on extreme/deviant cases because distinctive characteristics of extreme cases are often more obvious than in typical cases.
      (4) Can also be used to select participants from *both ends* of a continuum.
   e) Intensity Sampling
      (1) Select individuals who are likely to have intense experiences or feelings relating to the topic of research.
      (2) Difference from extreme/deviant sampling: Extreme sampling selects individuals who are different from most, while intensity sampling selects individuals who have more intense experiences.
   f) Maximum Variation Sampling
      (1) Cases selected so that full range of characteristics of interest is present in the sample.
      (2) Advantage: makes it possible to compare results across a wide spectrum of variables.
   g) Homogeneous Sampling
      (1) Opposite of maximum variation sampling.
      (2) Individuals selected based on similarities in important ways.
      (3) Narrows scope of a study.
   h) Opportunistic Sampling
      (1) Participants selected as the opportunity arises.
      (2) Difference from convenience sampling: Convenience sampling chooses cases only because they happen to be convenient, whereas opportunistic sampling may identify individuals as the opportunity arises, but they may not be at all convenient to study.
   i) Stratified Purposive Sampling
      (1) Subgroups of interest in the population must first be identified.

              (2) Participants from each subgroup must be selected so all subgroups are represented.

     j) Snowball Sampling

              (1) Initial participant(s) identifies additional participants for a study.

              (2) Two keys to snowball sampling:

- At least one individual with at least one additional contact must be located.
- Researcher must build rapport with the initial participants.

              (3) Can be used to locate information-rich individuals or those "hidden" or "hard to find."

     k) Combination Purposive Sampling

              (1) Sometimes desirable to use combination of various types of purposive sampling to obtain a single sample.

              (2) May use two or more types of samples and analyze the results separately for each type—allows research to identify similarities and differences between types of samples.

II. Improving Convenience Sampling

     a) If convenience sampling is the only option, researchers should try to obtain convenience samples from diverse sources.

     b) When used, demographic information should be collected so that the convenience sample can be described in detail.

III. Participant Recruitment in Qualitative Research

     a) Researchers use a variety of means to recruit participants.

     b) Proposed method of participant recruitment should be described in detail in a research proposal.

IV. Sample Size in Qualitative Research

     a) Samples used in qualitative research are often much smaller than samples used in quantitative research.

     b) Two factors that contribute to small sample size:

              (1) Qualitative researchers strive to purposively select individuals who are "information-rich."

              (2) Qualitative methods can require large amounts of time to be spent with each participant.

              (3) Saturation is important in determining sample size.

              (4) Beginning researchers should specify a target number, despite willingness to be open-ended regarding sample size.

Chapter 14: Measurement in Quantitative Research

I. Standardization and Objectivity of Measurement
    a) Quantitative researchers value *standardization*.
    b) Also value *objectivity*—an *objective test* can be scored without subjective judgment.
II. Social Desirability
    a) Participants tend to provide responses that they believe are desirable from a social point of view.
    b) To reduce influence of social desirability, assure participants that the information they provide is for research purposes only and only group statistics will be reported.
    c) Asking for anonymous responses to sensitive questions can also reduce it.
III. Reliability and Internal Consistency
    a) The Concept of Reliability in Measurement
        (1) Consistency is synonymous with reliability—researchers favor measure that yields consistent scores.
    b) Test-Retest Reliability
        (1) Determined by administering a test or other measure twice to a sample of examinees.
        (2) There will be some fluctuation from one administration to the next because of three factors:
            • Guessing on a test or making random marks in response to questions.
            • Changes in the physical and mental status of the examinees.
            • Changes in how the test was administered and testing conditions.
        (3) Reliability measured with a *reliability coefficient*—range from 0.00 (no consistency) to 1.00 (perfect consistency).
        (4) High reliabilities range from 0.85 and up.
    c) Internal Consistency
        (1) Refers to consistency of results from one part of a test or scale to another.
        (2) The result of correlating is called *split-half reliability coefficient*—ranges from 0.00 to 1.00.
        (3) In practice, the split-half technique is replaced with *Cronbach's alpha (α)*, which is mathematically equivalent to splitting a test over and over in many ways as possible.
        (4) If internal consistency is low, it could mean one of two things:
            • Scores may have been influenced by guessing or by examinees making random marks.
            • Scale or test measures more than one skill or trait.
    d) Interobserver Reliability
        (1) Refers to the extent to which two or more observers arrive at the same scores when they observe the behavior of the same participants.
        (2) Becomes important whenever observational process is not completely objective.
        (3) If interobserver reliability is low, it could mean one of two things:
            • The characteristic being observed is inherently difficult to judge.
            • One or more of the observers were careless or not properly trained in how to make the observations.
IV. Validity and Its Relationship to Reliability
    a) *Validity* refers to the extent to which a measure assesses what it is designed to measure.

       b)   Important to note: A test or scale can be highly reliable yet be invalid.

V. Judgmental Validity

       a)   Content Validity

           (1) Based on experts' judgments of the appropriateness of the contents of a scale or test for a particular purpose.

       b)   Face Validity

           (1) Assessment of validity based on nonexpert judgments of what a test appears to measure on the surface.

           (2) Researchers mainly concerned with content validity, not face validity.

           (3) Face validity can become a concern when examinees do not think that a test is valid and therefore refuse to take the test or fail to try their best.

           (4) More of a "public relations" concern.

VI. Criterion-Related Validity

       a)   Based on the extent to which scores on a test or scale correlate with scores on a criterion.

       b)   *Criterion* is a standard by which something can be judged.

       c)   Two types:

           (1) *Concurrent validity*—results when the test that is being validated is administered at about the same time as the criterion scores are being gathered.

           (2) *Predictive validity*—should be determined for all tests and scales that are designed to predict some future behavior.

       d)   Expressed with a *validity coefficient*—is mathematically calculated the same way as a reliability coefficient—ranges from 0.00 to 1.00.

       e)   Rough guidelines to help beginning researchers:

           (1) Coefficients below .20 = poor validity.

           (2) Coefficients between .20 and .39 = modest validity.

           (3) Coefficients between .40 and .60 = good validity.

           (4) Coefficients above .61 = excellent validity.

VII. Construct Validity

       a)   Refers to the extent to which a measure yields scores that are consistent with what is known (or generally believed to be true) about the construct it is designed to measure.

       b)   *Construct* is the label for a cohesive set of related behaviors.

Chapter 15: Writing Objective Measures

I.   Attitude Scales
   a) Planning an Attitude Scale
      (1) An *attitude* consists of *feelings* that have the potential to lead to *actions*.
      (2) When planning an attitude scale, first identify the component of the object of the attitudes.
      (3) Specify how many attitude scale items will be written for each component.
      (4) Plan to have an item or two that ask for overall attitudes.
   b) Writing an Attitude Scale
      (1) Basic concept of Likert scale is to write straightforward statements about the object of the attitude.
      (2) Likert scale choices vary from "Strongly Agree" to "Strongly Disagree."
      (3) Half of the statements should be favorable and half should be unfavorable.
      (4) *Reverse scoring* should be used for the items expressing unfavorable sentiments.
   c) Pilot Testing an Attitude Scale
      (1) A pilot test of the attitude scale items should be conducted with respondents who will not be included in the main study.
      (2) Use two techniques to get information on the quality of the items:
         • "Think aloud" technique.
         • Ask respondents to write notes in the margins on anything that bothers them or is unclear.

II. Observation Checklists
   a) Planning an Observation Checklist
      (1) Observation checklist consists of a list of behaviors and characteristics for which observations should be made.
      (2) Specific behaviors should be identified that are indicators of a particular trait.
      (3) The context within which the observations will be made should be put in writing in the plan.
   b) Writing an Observation Checklist
      (1) Each item in the observation checklist should refer to only a single, discrete behavior.
      (2) Observation checklists are frequently used to evaluate the performance of a task.
      (3) Can also include items that touch on *speed of behavior*, *duration of behavior*, and *success of the behavior*.
   c) Pilot Testing an Observation Checklist
      (1) Conduct the pilot test with participants who will not be included in the main study.
      (2) Key to success is to have two or more observers observe the same participants at the same time without conferring with each other.
      (3) Then, the extent to which the observers agree with each checklist item should be determined.
      (4) When disagreements arise, it helps if the researcher provides definitions.

III. Achievement Tests
   a) Planning an Achievement Test
      (1) Most popular type is the multiple-choice item.
      (2) Key to success is to base the test on the specific instructional objectives.
   b) Writing Achievement Test Items

          (1) A multiple-choice test item should have two or more *distracters*.

          (2) To prevent ambiguity in multiple-choice items, items should be written as clearly as possible.

    c) Pilot Testing an Achievement Test

          (1) Conduct the pilot test with participants who will not be included in the main study.

          (2) Calculate the percentage that marked each multiple-choice item correctly and examine the results for unexpected findings.

          (3) Can also gain useful information by comparing the performance of examinees that typically are high in achievement with that of examinees who are typically low in achievement.

IV. Concluding Comments

    a) Tests prepared by professionals usually undergo more expert and comprehensive reviews.

    b) Beginning researchers are advised to use measures previously developed by professionals when possible.

Chapter 16: Measurement in Qualitative Research

I. Issues in Interviewer Selection and Behavior
    a) Matching Interviewers and Participants
        (1) Interviewers need to be able to establish rapport with participants so that they will feel comfortable in being forthcoming with information.
        (2) Important consideration is the match of the background characteristics of the interviewer(s) and the participants.
    b) Interviewer Self-Disclosure
        (1) Interviewers should engage in *self-disclosure*—consciously thinking about their traits and beliefs that might affect their decisions.
        (2) Should take place before any interviews are conducted and should be noted in the report of the research.
II. Devising Interview Protocols
    a) Semi-Structured, Open-Ended Interviews
        (1) Often used by qualitative researchers.
        (2) Protocol can take two forms:
            • Can have a core set of questions to be asked of all participants while allowing the interviewers to add additional questions as needed.
            • Can be less formal, consisting of only a list of topics about which questions will be asked.
        (3) Probes are helpful when participants provide vague or general answers.
        (4) Qualitative researchers typically use *open-ended questions*.
    b) Initial Questions to Establish Rapport
        (1) Initial questions asked set the tone for the rest of an interview.
        (2) Care should be taken to use initial questions to make the participants feel comfortable.
    c) Using Previously Developed Interview Protocols
        (1) Using previously developed protocols measure more characteristics of quantitative research than qualitative research.
    d) Having Interview Protocols Reviewed
        (1) Always a good idea to have your interview protocol reviewed by experts whenever possible.
        (2) Especially important for beginning researchers.
    e) Pilot Testing Interview Protocols
        (1) Less crucial for qualitative research to pilot test a measure because it is acceptable for qualitative researchers to modify their measures as they collect data.
        (2) A pilot test may help beginning researchers with the opportunity to practice their interviewing skills.
    f) Formulating Questions about Demographics
        (1) Questions asking for demographic information should be standardized for all participants.
        (2) Potentially sensitive questions should usually be asked near the end of the interview.
        (3) When asking sensitive questions, interviewers should preface them with a brief explanation for asking them.

(4) To soften the impact of sensitive questions, interviewers can offer choices that cover ranges rather than asking for specific numbers (as in age or income).

g) Recording Responses and Note Taking

    (1) Advantage to recording: produces a complete record of participants' responses.

    (2) Disadvantage to recording: presence of a recorder might inhibit some participants.

    (3) Alternative to recording is to take notes.

- Two major disadvantages:
    i. Notes will not constitute a complete record of responses.
    ii. Greatly complicates the work of the interviewers.

    (4) Beginning researchers should record responses instead of making notes, unless dealing with highly sensitive matters.

    (5) Always make notes of important aspects of the interview as soon as possible after the conclusion of each interview.

Part D
Techniques for Data Analysis

Chapter 17: Descriptive Statistics for Quantitative and Qualitative Research

I. Describing Nominal Data
    a) *Nominal data* refers to data that consist of names or labels that contain words, not numbers.
    b) *Percentage* indicates how many participants out of 100 have some trait or characteristic.
    c) Can examine the relationship between two nominal variables by building a *contingency table*.

II. Describing Ordinal Data
    a) *Ordinal data* put participants in rank order from high to low.
    b) Can be summarized with the *median* and *interquartile range*.

III. Describing Ratio and Interval Data
    a) Three characteristics of *ratio data*:
        (1) Tell "how much" of a characteristic each participant has.
        (2) All units represent the same amount of the characteristic.
        (3) Ratio data have a true, absolute zero point.
    b) *Interval data* have first two characteristics of ratio data.
        (1) However, they do not have a true zero.
        (2) A zero on an objective test often is arbitrary (not absolute).
    c) The Mean and Median
        (1) *Mean*—most commonly used descriptive statistic for averaging ratio and interval data.
          • Computationally, it is the average obtained by summing all the scores and dividing by the number of scores.
          • The symbols for the mean are *M* (used if the data are for an entire population) and *m* (if the data are for only a sample drawn from a population).
        (2) Major drawback for certain data sets—if there are some extreme scores on one side of a distribution without extreme scores on the other side, the mean may be pulled too far toward the extreme to be representative of the typical participant.
        (3) *Skewed*—when the distribution is unbalanced.
        (4) Two ways to handle the problem of skewed results: calculate the mean with and without the extreme cases with an explanation that the distribution is skewed and report the *median*.
        (5) *Median*—always the score with 50% of the cases above it and 50% below it.
    d) The Standard Deviation and Interquartile Range
        (1) *Standard deviation*—most always used to describe variation when the mean has been used as the average.
          • The larger the variation, the larger the standard deviation will be.
          • In published reports, the symbols often used are *SD* (when describing a whole population) and *sd* (when describing a sample from a population).
          • Designed to describe *normal distribution (bell-shaped curve)*.
        (2) Use *interquartile range* for a highly skewed distribution instead of the mean.
          • *Interquartile range*—the range of a middle of 50% of the scores.

Chapter 18: Correlational Statistics for Quantitative Research

I. Correlational methods allow researchers to examine and describe relationships between pairs of scores for a group of participants.
    a) Correlation coefficients provide a precise number to express the strength of a relationship.
        (1) Can range from 1.00 (for a direct relationship with no exceptions) to 0.00 (for the absence of a relationship).
        (2) Has a positive value for *direct relationships* (*positive relationships*) and has a negative value for *inverse relationships* (*negative relationships*).
    b) Most widely used correlation coefficient is the *Pearson product-moment correlation coefficient* (*Pearson r*).
    c) Correlation coefficients describe two characteristics of a relationship:
        (1) Whether a relationship is direct or inverse.
        (2) The strength of the trend.

II. Describing the Strength of a Relationship
    a) A value of a Pearson *r* that is very close to 1.00 would be described as a "very strong" direct relationship.
    b) A value of a Pearson *r* that is very close to -1.00 would be described as a "very strong" inverse relationship.
    c) A positive value of a Pearson *r* that is very close to 0.00 would be described as a "very weak" direct relationship.
    d) A negative value of a Pearson *r* that is very close to 0.00 would be described as "very weak" inverse relationship

Chapter 19: Inferential Statistics for Quantitative Research

I.   *Inferential statistics* are used by researchers who have sampled from a population.
II. Margins of Error
    a) Based primarily on the number of participants. The larger the sample of participants, the lower the margin of error will be.
    b) Must have some degree of confidence associated with it.
III. The Null Hypothesis
    a) *Null hypothesis*—states that a difference may have been created by errors caused by random sampling.
    b) These errors are called *sampling errors.*
    c) Research hypotheses state what researchers predict they will find, whereas null hypothesis always asserts that the difference may be created by sampling errors.
IV. The Chi-Square Test
    a) *Chi-square test*—test of the null hypothesis involving differences among percentages.
    b) Establishes a probability that the null hypothesis is a correct hypothesis.
    c) In social and behavioral sciences, any probability of 5 or less in 100 is usually regarded as sufficiently low to reject the null hypothesis.
    d) When the null hypothesis has been rejected based on an inferential statistical test, researchers declare the difference to be *statistically significant.*
    e) The symbol for Chi Square is χ^2, and the symbol for probability is *p*.
V.   The *t* Test
    a) The *t* Test for Means
        (1) *t* test—used to obtain the probability that sampling error created the difference between 2 means.
        (2) Can be used to test the difference between only one pair of means at a time.
    b) The *t* Test for Correlation Coefficients
        (1) When a correlation coefficient is based on a sample from a population, the null hypothesis says that there is no true correlation.
        (2) Customary to omit the value of *t* when reporting the significance of a correlation coefficient.
VI. The *F* Test (ANOVA)
    a) *F* test is an extension of the *t* test.
    b) Conducted using a set of procedures known as Analysis of Variance (ANOVA).
    c) Significant value of *F* only indicates that the set of differences as a whole probably has some nonrandom differences.
    d) To determine which specific pairs of means are significantly different from each other, use *multiple comparisons test.*
VII. Statistical Versus Practical Significance
    a) Statistical significance indicates only that whatever difference(s) is/are being considered is/are unlikely to have been created at random—not necessarily of any practical significance.
    b) Three considerations for practical significance:
        (1) Consider *cost in relation to benefit* to determine practical significance.
        (2) Consider whether statistically significant results suggest actions that are questionable from an ethical or legal standpoint.
        (3) Consider *acceptability*.

Chapter 20: A Closer Look at Data Analysis in Qualitative Research

I. Self-Disclosure and Bracketing in Data Analysis
   a) Individuals collecting data should engage in *self-disclosure*.
   b) Self-disclosure should be followed by *bracketing*—refers to setting aside any individual's beliefs and concerns in order to be able to view the phenomena under investigation from the point of view of the participants.
II. A Closer Look at the Grounded Theory Approach
   a) Three stages of coding in the grounded theory approach:
      (1) Open coding—distinct, separate segments of the responses of participants are identified and given names.
      (2) Axial coding—creation of *categories*, higher order labels that encompass several concepts.
      (3) Selective coding—develops a *core category* and describes the process by which variables interact and are related to each other.
III. A Closer Look at the Consensual Qualitative Approach
   a) Consensual Qualitative Research (CQR) emphasizes reaching consensus, so researchers must establish how and when the consensus-building process will be conducted.
   b) Steps in CQR method:
      (1) Code into domains—refers to segmenting the data into groups according to the topics they cover.
      (2) Develop core ideas within domains—write short summaries that reduce the original idea of participants into fewer words.
      (3) Have domains and core ideas developed in the first two steps audited by an outside expert.
      (4) Cross-analysis—core ideas are grouped into categories based on similarities.
      (5) Stability check—done by examining additional data, if available.

Issues in Conducting Surveys
Chapter 21: Issues in Participant Selection for Surveys

I. Surveys—type of nonexperimental, quantitative research.
   a) Two major sources of bias in surveys: using the postal system to conduct direct mail surveys and using the Internet to conduct email and online surveys.

II. Participant Issues in Conducting Direct Mail Surveys
   a) Often most efficient way to reach respondents who reside in geographically diverse locations is via postal service.
   b) Researchers use various techniques to increase response rates to direct mail surveys:
      (1) Offer an incentive, such as a physical reward.
      (2) Personalize the survey by having the questionnaires mailed by a person or agency that the potential respondents will recognize.
      (3) Send successive mailings of a questionnaire to nonrespondents.
   c) Additional steps listed to improve response rates:
      (1) Enclose a self-addressed, stamped envelope.
      (2) Keep vocabulary and grammar as simple as possible.
      (3) Avoid using technical jargon in questions designed for the general public.
      (4) Keep questionnaire as short as possible.
      (5) Point out how the results will directly benefit the participants.

III. Participant Issues in Conducting Internet Surveys
   a) Email surveys work best when the researcher has only a few simple questions to ask.
   b) Online surveys
      (1) Potential respondents click on a link in an email that takes them to a survey.
      (2) Response rates to online surveys can vary dramatically.
      (3) Biased against individuals and households that do not have access to the Internet. Individuals with modest incomes or education are less likely to use the Internet.

IV. Techniques for Improving Convenience Samples
   a) Consider Adjusting the Research Problem
      (1) May want to adjust the research purpose in light of the accessibility of potential participants.
   b) Use Diverse Locations and Times
   c) Use Population Demographics When Planning the Sample
      (1) Office of institutional research on most campuses routinely compiles demographic information on the student body—often available to the public.
      (2) Can be used by researchers who are trying to draw a representative sample of a study body.
   d) Use Population Demographics When Analyzing the Data
   e) Track Information on Nonvolunteers
      (1) Nonvolunteers—participants who were contacted but refused to participate.
      (2) The differential in rates of participation should be noted in the research report in order to advise readers of a potential bias in sampling.
   f) Consider Seeking a Community-Based Sample
      (1) Can be obtained by soliciting participation in public places.
      (2) Additionally, community groups and organizations might provide access to their members: social clubs, religious institutions, and neighborhood councils.

V. Concluding Comment
   a) Obtaining a representative sample is more important than using a large sample.
   b) It is better to work with a smaller representative sample than a larger biased sample.

Chapter 22: Issues in Measuring Demographics in Surveys

I. Determining Which Demographics to Collect
    a) Almost limitless types of demographic information that might be collected.
    b) Only demographics deemed to be relevant to the research problem should be collected.

II. Writing Demographic Questions
    a) Questions on Sensitive Variables
        (1) Mitigate impact of potentially sensitive matters by providing a range of values from which participants may choose.
        (2) Be sure to include exhaustive choices when presenting a range of values.
        (3) Consider how many individuals are likely to fall into each range.
        (4) Racial and ethnic background are potentially sensitive issues.
            • Preferred terms change over time and various members of the same group may prefer different terms.
            • Provide alternative terms and a choice for "Other" to allow participants to indicate mixed ancestry.
        (5) Helpful to examine how professional survey researchers have written items on race/ethnicity.
    b) Providing Definitions
        (1) Determine if definitions or explanations for terms in demographic questions should be provided.
        (2) Important to provide definitions when using technical terms.
    c) Providing Exhaustive Choices
        (1) Choices in an item should be exhaustive—providing a choice for each possibility.
        (2) Sometimes difficult to spot deficiencies in the exhaustiveness of the choices.
    d) Providing Spaces for Responses to Open-Ended Questions
        (1) Choices that participants can quickly check off should be provided.
        (2) Some items may have so many possible choices that providing choices would be unwieldy (e.g., zip codes).
        (3) Be sure to provide an adequate amount of space for open-ended items.

III. Pilot Testing Demographic Questions
    a) Pilot test individuals who will not be participating in the main survey.
    b) To get feedback, ask each individual to "think aloud" as they consider and respond to the questions.

IV. Organizing and Introducing Demographic Questions
    a) All demographic items should be grouped together and placed at the end of the questionnaire or schedule.
    b) Give a brief explanation for asking demographic information. This helps blunt resistance to answering questions that some participants might view as invasive of their privacy.

Chapter 23: Issues in the Use of Questionnaires in Surveys

I. Preparing Instruments for Administration
    a) Give a Questionnaire a Title
        (1) Clearly indicate the types of variables covered.
        (2) Be as clear and specific as possible.
    b) Prepare an Introduction
        (1) Brief introduction should indicate:
- The purpose of the survey.
- The sponsor.
- The approximate amount of time it will take to complete the questionnaire.
- Whether responses will remain confidential.

        (2) Point out any potential benefits that might accrue either to the individual responding or to some group of individuals.
    c) Group the Items by Topic
        (1) Group items by topic if there is more than one question in each of several subtopics.
        (2) Provide subheadings for each group.
    d) Conclude with a "Thank You" and provide contact information
        (1) Instrument should end with a thank you statement.
        (2) Participants should be informed of how to contact the researcher in the future.

II. Group Administration of Questionnaires
    a) When surveying a group, potential participants should be given the right to decline to participate.
    b) Advantage of Group Administration
        (1) Efficient way to obtain a large sample.
    c) Disadvantage of Group Administration
        (1) Clusters tend to be homogeneous in important respects.
        (2) Responses from clusters may not represent the full diversity of participants.

III. Individual Administration of Questionnaires
    a) Advantage of Individual Administration
        (1) Will usually provide a more diverse sample.
    b) Disadvantage of Individual Administration
        (1) Takes more effort and time.
    c) Advantages of Face-to-Face Administration
        (1) Participation rates can be higher when participants are approached on a face-to-face basis.
        (2) Researchers might get insights into participants' understanding of the questions through comments and facial expressions.

Part F
Issues in Conducting Experiments

Chapter 24: Introduction to Experimentation and Threats to External Validity

I. Experiments Explore Cause-and-Effect Relationships
   a) Set of treatments is called the *independent variable*.
   b) The outcome variable is called the *dependent variable*.
II. Controlling the Hawthorne Effect in Experimentation
   a) Refers to the tendency of participants to improve because they are being studied.
   b) Can use an *attention control group* to control for this.
III. Using Multiple Independent and Dependent Variables
   a) A given experiment can have more than one independent variable (more than one set of treatments).
   b) By examining two independent variables at the same time in the same experiment, can examine how the variables work together to produce difference on the dependent variable—called can *interaction* of the independent variables.
   c) Number of dependent variables limited only by the number of outcomes that might reasonably be expected to be influenced by the independent variable and the willingness of participants to complete multiple measures.
IV. External Validity of Experiments
   a) Refers to the ability to generalize results of an experiment in a population.
   b) Five threats to external validity:
      (1) Selection Bias
         • Refers to any bias that might have occurred in the selection of individuals to be participants.
         • Random selection is key to preventing bias in sampling.
      (2) Reactive Effects of Experimental Arrangements
         • Setting of experimental research can have an effect on how the participants respond to treatments.
         • Can occur whenever anything about the experimental setting is unlike the natural setting in which the behavior ordinarily occurs.
      (3) Reactive Effects of Testing
         • Refers to the possibility that the pretest in an experiment might sensitize participants to a treatment.
         • Can avoid by using *unobtrusive measures*.
      (4) Obtrusiveness of Measurement
         • Measurement might obtrude on participants and cause them to react differently than they would if there were no measurement.
         • To avoid, can use *unobtrusive measures*.
            a. Can often be used in field experiments through observation at a distance or indirect observation.
      (5) Multiple-Treatment Interference
         • Occurs when the same participant is given more than one treatment.
V. Concluding Comments
   a) An experiment is said to have good external validity when it is reasonable to believe that the results apply to a population in a natural setting.
   b) Not possible to avoid all threats, but steps should be taken to eliminate as many as possible.

Chapter 25: Threats to Internal Validity and True Experiments

I. An experiment is said to have good internal validity if it is conducted in such a way that the independent variable is the only viable explanation for changes observed in participants.

II. History

    a) Refers to any event external to the experiment that might have caused the observed change in participants' behavior.

    b) Controlling History with a True Experiment

        (1) Can be controlled by conducting *true experiments*.

        (2) All true experiments have more than one group of participants, and the participants are assigned to groups at random.

        (3) Basic true experiment has two groups with pretests and posttests for each group.

        (4) True experimental design controls for history by having a control group that will be influenced by the same external events.

III. Maturation

    a) Refers to natural developmental changes—most noticeable in young children.

    b) Can be controlled by conducting a true experiment.

IV. Instrumentation

    a) Refers to possible changes in a measure or measurement process.

    b) Within a true experiment, both the experimental and control group would tend to change from pretest to posttest at the same rate because of instrumentation.

V. Testing

    a) Results from learning how to take a particular test with the result that performances are increased on the posttest—sometimes called *practice effect*.

    b) Can be controlled by conducting a true experiment.

VI. Statistical Regression

    a) Refers to the tendency of participants who are extremely high or extremely low to score closer to the mean on retesting—extremes tend to correct themselves.

    b) Can be controlled by conducting a true experiment—if extreme scores are randomly assigned, both groups will be likely to regress toward the mean at the same rate.

VII. Selection

    a) Happens when two (or more) nonequivalent groups are compared.

    b) Whenever nonrandom assignment is used to form the experimental and control groups, groups are presumed to be nonequivalent.

    c) Can be prevented by forming the two groups at random.

VIII. True Experimental Designs

    a) True experimental design can easily be extended to have more than two groups.

    b) Equivalency is the result of random assignment, not the pretest.

        (1) Not necessary to have a pretest in order to have a true experiment.

        (2) Not having a pretest avoids threat to external validity called "reactive effects of testing."

        (3) Advantage of having a pretest in the amount of growth or change can be determined from the beginning of an experiment to the end on the posttest.

IX. Concluding Comments

    a) By using a true experiment, all the above threats to internal validity are controlled.

Chapter 26: Pre-Experiments and Quasi-Experiments

I. Pre-Experiments
- a) Can be thought of as an activity that is done before formal experimentation begins.
- b) The three pre-experiment designs are so weak that they are of almost no value in exploring cause-and-effect relationships:
  - (1) First example—has only one group of participants who were given a pretest, followed by a treatment, followed by a posttest.
  - (2) One-shot case study—has only one group that is given a treatment, followed by a test—there is no pretest.
    - Because there is no pretest, it is impossible to know if there has even been any change in the participants.
    - Subject to all the threats to internal validity—essentially of no value for exploring cause-and-effect relationships.
  - (3) Static-group comparison design—both an experimental and control group receive a posttest, but no pretest.
- c) Some beginning researchers might use pre-experimental designs in a preliminary pilot test prior to beginning a more formal experiment—can help improve tests and other observational methods.

II. Quasi-Experimental
- a) The three types of quasi-experiments, while not as good as true experimental designs, they are still of some value for exploring cause-and-effect relationships:
  - (1) Non-equivalent control group design—has an experimental group that receives the treatment, and a control group.
    - Individuals are not assigned at random, but instead are preexisting groups—most useful when the pretest scores are similar for the two groups.
    - Key problem: no matter how similar the two groups are known to be at time of pretest, they may differ in some systematic way that is unknown to the researcher.
  - (2) Time-series design—conducted with one group of participants.
    - Most useful when the dependent variable is a variable that naturally fluctuates from time to time without any special treatment.
    - A series of pretests are called *baseline*.
  - (3) Equivalent time samples design—involves only one group of participants.
    - Some days treatment is given, some days it is not—days for the treatment are selected at random.
    - Key problem: threat to external validity called "multiple-treatment interference.

III. Concluding Comments
- a) For most experimental purposes, true experimental designs are most desirable.
- b) If random assignment is not possible, quasi-experimental designs might be used to obtain useful information.
- c) As a rule, pre-experimental designs should be avoided except when used as preliminary pilot studies conducted prior to formal experimentation to refine treatments and measures.

Chapter 27: Writing Reports of Empirical Research

I. Research proposals can be used as the foundation of a research report.
   a) Major sections include: Title, Introduction, Literature Review, Method (with subheadings Participants, Measures, and Procedures), Results, Discussion, and References.
   b) Title should be a brief statement that names the major variables in the research hypothesis, purpose, or question.
II. The Abstract
   a) Brief summary that is placed below the title—typically 150 words or less, unless a thesis or dissertation which may be longer.
   b) At a minimum should indicate:
      (1) The general purpose of the research.
      (2) The types of individuals who served as participants.
      (3) The general nature of the results.
III. The Introduction and Literature Review
   a) Purpose of literature review:
      (1) To establish the context for the research study.
      (2) To justify the study by establishing that the problem area is important.
   b) If an introduction or literature review is more than two or three double-spaced pages, consider using subheadings.
IV. The Method Section
   a) Almost always has a subsection on participants and a subsection on measures.
   b) A subsection on procedures is often desirable—needed whenever there are important physical steps that were taken in order to conduct the research that were not fully described under the other subheadings.
V. The Results Section
   a) Some researchers provide demographic information in the subsection on participants, but others summarize the demographic data at the beginning of the Results section.
   b) When writing the Results section, keep in mind that no matter how strong the trends in data are, they are subject to errors.
   c) It is *always* inappropriate to use the term "prove." Instead, refer to the degree of confidence in the results based on the evidence provided by the data.
   d) Qualitative results are typically much longer than quantitative results because they are expressed in words and must be justified.
VI. The Discussion Section
   a) Often begins with a brief summary of the preceding material in the research report.
   b) Should state the general purpose of the study and indicate the major results—also helpful to indicate whether the major results are consistent with those discussed earlier in the literature review.
   c) Summary is typically followed by a discussion of the limitations (weaknesses) of the study. This protects researchers from being charged with naively failing to recognize weaknesses.
   d) Special strengths of the study should be pointed out.
   e) Also include suggestions for future research—be as specific as possible.
VII. References
   a) Should be placed immediately after the discussion.
   b) Pay attention to details when formatting references.

Learning Resource 3

Conducting Research Online: Challenges Facing Researchers

A substantial number of consumers and their families now have access to e-mail and the Internet. According to the UCLA Center for Communication Policy (2003), more than 70% of Americans used the Internet in 2003, with e-mail cited as the most common online activity. The growth in e-mail and Internet usage makes online methodologies appealing for conducting research, especially in Family and Consumer Sciences (FCS).

There are several reasons why FCS researchers might be interested in using an online survey to conduct research. First, online survey techniques can provide access to populations that are difficult to reach with traditional survey methods. These populations might include, but are not limited to, those unlikely to participate in face-to-face research activities because of societal stigmas, work or family commitments, or the inconveniences and other constraints associated with traditional survey methods (Andrews, Nonnecke, & Preece, 2003; Murray & Fisher, 2002). The Internet can provide a sense of social distance for some target populations, resulting in more open responses in online surveys than in other data collection methods. The Internet also can be a convenient way to participate for those with computer experience and a preference for completing the survey at their leisure. Greater access to, and knowledge of, hard-to-reach populations result in samples that are more representative of the general population.

From a practical standpoint, online surveys have several other advantages over traditional mail and telephone surveys. In general, the benefits of conducting online surveys range from potentially larger sample sizes and faster response rates to less data processing and lower costs (Bachmann, Elfrink, & Vazzana, 2000; Jackson & DeCormier, 1999; McDonald & Adam, 2003; Mehta & Sivades, 1995). Online surveys can be delivered in a matter of seconds and have been reported to have faster turnaround times and fewer respondent errors. Also, the process of sending e-mails and setting up online surveys is less expensive than conducting mail and telephone surveys. In many cases, online surveys can reduce the marginal costs of data collection to zero because researchers avoid the costs associated with printing and mailing the survey and including return postage. Cobanoglu, Warde, and Moreo (2001) reported a mean response period of 5.97 days for online surveys compared to 16.46 days for mail surveys; they also estimated the total costs for a mail survey at 2.4 times the costs of a comparable online survey.

Besides these advantages, there are also a number of challenges with respect to the validity, design, and implementation of online surveys. The purpose of this article is to highlight the opportunities associated with online surveying while being realistic about the challenges that FCS researchers are likely to face when using this research methodology. This article seeks to minimize the extent to which FCS researchers repeat the errors of their predecessors by providing, whenever possible, specific examples from previous FCS studies. Essentially, this article is a primer for those with limited or no experience in using online surveying methods.

Online Research in Family and Consumer Sciences

The use of online surveys is relatively new to researchers and practitioners in the field of FCS. Yet FCS researchers increasingly are using online methods to collect data on a wide range of topics and from a variety of target populations, including online shoppers, students, financial practitioners, employees, and investors.

It is important to note that there are two techniques that one can use to conduct studies using the Internet. The first uses e-mail and is akin to traditional mail surveys; the respondent receives an e-mail with the survey either embedded in the e-mail or included as an attachment that the respondent opens and completes. In the other technique, a survey is posted to a website, respondents are directed to the site using e-mail or another method, and information is collected and downloaded at the site. In this article, the latter technique is referred to as an online survey, whereas e-mail surveys are referred to as such. This article focuses primarily on online surveys because this tends to be the method most FCS researchers have chosen. The following sections provide specific examples that highlight some of the ways in which FCS researchers have used online surveying techniques effectively to conduct research. The specific details of FCS studies also are included throughout the article wherever relevant.

Researchers in family and consumer economics have conducted a number of studies online. Several used online surveys to investigate Internet purchasing behaviors. For example, Cude and Morganosky (2000; Morganosky & Cude, 2002) used online surveys to collect data from online grocery shoppers to learn more about who purchases groceries online, how much they spend, and how frequently they make purchases. Kwon and Lee (2003) used data from an Internet survey administered by the Georgia Institute of Technology Graphics Visualization and Usability Center to investigate online shoppers' concerns about Internet payment security.

A number of other family and consumer economics researchers used online surveys to examine the financial decisions and practices of various target populations. Volpe, Kotel, and Chen (2002) collected data to determine whether online investors' levels of investment literacy varied by their characteristics, and Hanna, Gutter, and Fan (2001) used online survey techniques to investigate an improved subjective measure of risk tolerance. More recently, researchers in family and consumer economics used online surveys to collect data from college students, in particular on their credit practices and financial education needs (i.e., Lawrence et al., 2003; Lyons, 2003, 2004; Pollack, Foster, & Robinson, 2004).

Examples of online surveys also can be found in child and family development. Birnbaum (2004) cited a number of studies in social and cognitive psychology that used online methods to conduct experiments, often examining whether online and laboratory experiments yielded the same results. Other researchers examined online social behaviors. Nosek, Banaji, and Greenwald (2002) focused on whether individuals exhibit different social behaviors online versus in person, whereas Cooper, Morahan-Martin, Mathy, and Maheu (2002) conducted a study through the MSNBC website to learn more about people who engage in online sexual activity.

Some researchers have used online methods to examine various aspects of family life. Colvin, Chenoweth, Bold, and Harding (2004) studied the perceptions that caregivers of older adults have of online social support networks. Hill, Hawkins, and Miller (1996) examined the impact of working from home on traditional work and family life using an IBM program to conduct an online survey of IBM employees. Moorefield and Proulx (2004) used the Internet to collect qualitative information on the family structure of gay couples.

Online surveys are also part of an emerging area of research in health and nutrition. Daley, McDermott, McCormack-Brown, and Kittleson (2003) used the Internet to collect data from college students and investigated the relationship between temperament type and health-risk-taking behavior among college students.

Vereecken (2001) also used an Internet survey to study the health behaviors of school-aged children in Belgium. Other researchers have used online surveys to assess how online education and support groups can improve patient outcomes, especially for those with diabetes (i.e., Anderson, Donnelly, & Hess, 1992; Farris, Stoupa, Mendenhall, & Mazzuca, 1994; McKay, King, Eakin, Seeley, & Glasgow, 2001; Meadows et al., 1988).

A few studies in FCS have focused on the technical aspects of online surveying and compared the effectiveness of Internet surveys to traditional mail, telephone, and/or fax surveys. Cobanoglu et al. (2001) compared the response speeds, response rates, and costs for mail, fax, and Web-based surveys using a random sample of hospitality professors from the Council on Hotel, Restaurant, and Institutional Education. They found that Web surveys by far had a faster response speed and higher response rate and were significantly cheaper than mail surveys. Litvin and Kar (2001) used a survey instrument to collect tourism research data by two independent collection methods: (1) a mall-intercept approach asking individuals who were passing through a mass-rapid transit station or shopping mall to participate and (2) an e-survey in which participants were sent an e-mail with the survey instrument attached as a document. They found that e-surveying was a viable means to conduct tourism research that resulted in a fairly representative sample of travelers. Overall, these studies, as well as others (i.e., Baruch, 1999; Gosling, Vazire, & Srivastava, 2004; Joinson, 2001; Reips, 2002; Wharton, Hampl, Hall, & Winham, 2003), provide evidence that online research methods can be, in specific and appropriate cases, more practical and desirable than traditional survey methods.

The remainder of this article focuses on the process of how to conduct an online survey and the challenges FCS researchers are likely to encounter, such as those associated with sampling, survey design, and data storage and confidentiality. A flow chart has been included to outline the process used by FCS researchers to conduct online survey research (see Table 1 on next page).

When an Online Survey is Appropriate

As previously mentioned, one of the major advantages to using online surveys to conduct FCS research is that they can be an effective means to collect data from hard-to-reach populations (Andrews et al., 2003; Murray & Fisher, 2002). In addition, a number of FCS studies provide evidence that the Internet can create a sense of social distance for some target populations, resulting in more open responses. Thus, researchers who need to ask questions that are more sensitive in nature, such as about illegal drug use or sexual behaviors, may obtain higher response rates using online

TABLE 1:   Flow Chart for Conducting an Online Survey

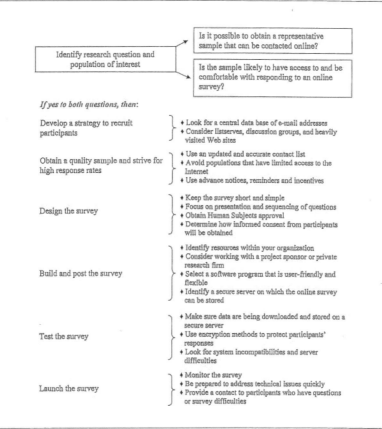

surveys than traditional paper surveys (Daley et al., 2003). Vereecken (2001) found that school-aged children were more likely to report having experimented with smoking, drinking alcohol, and skipping school in an online survey than in a paper survey. In addition, Moorefield and Proulx (2004) found that the breadth and depth of content collected from gay couples about their family structure increased when they used the Internet rather than face-to-face methods to collect data.

However, no matter which group is targeted, it is critical that researchers determine the degree to which the target population is likely to have access to a computer and the Internet (Katz & Aspden, 1997; McDonald & Adam, 2003; Stanton & Rogelberg, 2001; Taylor, 2000; Wilson & Laskey, 2003). Some target audiences with access, including teenagers, college students, "in house" employee groups, and professional or business groups, may respond better to online surveys than to traditional methods (Birnbaum, 2004). However, a significant fraction of U.S. households still do not have access to the Internet, and researchers must keep this in mind.

Some FCS researchers and practitioners are interested in populations that have more limited access to the Internet than the general public and will be less

able and willing to respond online (Stanton & Rogelberg, 2001; Taylor, 2000). The Pew Internet and American Life Project (Lenhart, 2003) reported that in 2003 those less likely to go online were more likely to be older, to be a member of a minority group, and to have modest incomes and education. One half of all nonusers were older than age 50, and one quarter did not have a high school diploma. Fifty-eight percent of all Americans went online compared to 8% of African Americans, 9% of Hispanics, and 18% of those with incomes less than $30,000. In rural areas, fewer than one half of Americans went online. In addition, nearly 30% of nonusers were retired and 16% were unemployed. Nonusers also were more likely to be disabled; 26% of nonusers reported a disability, compared to 12% of Internet users. The UCLA Center for Communication Policy (2003) found that Internet nonusers cited lack of technology (28% had no computer) and lack of interest (28%) as the primary reasons for not being online.

In addition to considering respondents' access to the Internet, researchers also must assess the level of comfort that the target population has with using a computer and the Internet. Many of the target populations that FCS researchers and practitioners might survey online have easy access to a computer and the Internet and would have the technical skills to respond to an online survey. These populations would include those that regularly complete transactions online (i.e., reservations, banking, investing, and shopping) and those who use a computer and the Internet for work or school.

Thus, although online surveys can be useful in reaching some groups, they are not appropriate for all target populations, especially low-income families, some minority groups, and elderly populations. Using online surveys inappropriately to target these populations can result in low response rates, nonresponse bias to survey questions, and ultimately, samples that are not representative of the target population (see the following sections for further details). Thus, researchers must use caution to determine whether an online survey is the appropriate research method and focus on populations that have both access to, and the ability to use, online technologies.

Recruitment of Participants

To conduct an online survey, researchers face a number of issues related to securing a sample. First and foremost, there is the issue of how to get the information needed to contact the target population. Researchers may find it difficult to gain contact information for some target populations, such as online shoppers and investors, as there is no centralized database of e-mail addresses (Litvin & Kar, 2001). In these cases, researchers must use alternative methods, such as electronic subscription groups, Internet discussion groups, and/or heavily visited websites, to gain access to their samples. Recall that Cooper et al. (2002) collected data through a survey on the MSNBC website. Colvin et al. (2004) recruited participants using Internet-based announcements on 15 different websites in the United States and Canada that offered caregiver online networks. Volpe et al. (2002) posted on investment-related message boards and contacted investment clubs to encourage their members to participate. Other researchers have successfully posted invitations on company websites that receive high traffic from target populations (Cude & Morganosky, 2000; Hill et al., 1996; Morganosky & Cude, 2002).

For those who want to obtain a more random sample of e-mail addresses from the general population, several free-access, commercial e-mail directories are available on the Internet (i.e., Yahoo or Switchboard). Litvin and Kar (2001) randomly selected 2,000 names from a telephone directory. They used a free-access e-mail directory to find an e-mail address for each name selected (see Litvin & Kar, 2001, for more details).

Other populations, including college and university students, employees, and members of specific organizations, also can be contacted through a central e-mail list. However, there are several issues to consider when using an existing e-mail list. One is the quality of the list. Individuals, especially students, frequently change their e-mail addresses and sometimes have more than one address. Before using an e-mail list, it is important to determine how frequently it is updated. If the updating is periodic, notices to the list ideally should be sent shortly after the most recent updating.

If the researcher can secure an e-mail list that was recently updated and accurately reflects the target population, then the sampling process may be fairly easy. The researcher can send an e-mail survey to respondents or an e-mail directing respondents to the website where the survey is posted. Certain office suites or stand-alone software, such as Campaign Enterprise 8, can simplify e-mail management and mail merging. Such software can use e-mail lists to send out personalized e-mails to part or all of the provided e-mail list. The software also can be used to track those who want to be removed from the list.

The last point brings up an important and emerging issue in online survey research. Many universities, employers, and other organizations increasingly are concerned about protecting personal privacy and may be hesitant to release a list of e-mail addresses for fear the information may be misused. They also are concerned that members will perceive the messages as "spam" and not want to be contacted. Definitions of "spam" vary, but in general, it refers broadly to any unsolicited bulk e-mail (or "junk" mail), which can be either commercial (i.e., an advertisement to promote a product or service) or noncommercial (i.e., an irrelevant message or chain letter). While conducting her study among college students, Lyons (2003) discovered that researchers could increase the probability of access to a central e-mail list by recommending that the administration send the e-mails. Under this condition, students were less likely to view the e-mail as spam.

Researchers should note that a company or organization is more likely to provide access to an e-mail list or an online directory of members if it believes the information being collected is of benefit to its clients or members. Often, researchers also must provide a solid argument as to how the research addresses an issue of importance to the population and how the population will benefit from the research. Given this, it is critical that researchers build relationships with the individuals, companies, and/or organizations they are interested in surveying. More often than not, online research that targets a specific population such as shoppers or investors was made possible because a researcher knew someone at a particular company or organization (i.e., Cude & Morganosky, 2000; Morganosky & Cude, 2002).

Regardless of how the list of participants is obtained (i.e., central database, listservs, discussion groups, or company directory), the quality of the sample primarily is determined by the quality of the list. Researchers need to have a list that is frequently updated and accurately reflects the target population.

Sampling and Response Rates

Online surveys can be particularly effective when researchers want to study a specific group rather than a
360 general cross-section of the population. However, collecting a broad and representative sample of the population of interest via the Internet is a challenge, particularly when some demographic groups are more likely to have limited access to the Internet (see Birnbaum,
365 2004; Selwyn & Robson, 1998; Solomon, 2001). It should not be surprising that response rates to online surveys tend to be lower for those with limited access to the Internet such as the elderly, poor, disabled, immigrants, and some ethnic groups (i.e., Katz & Aspden,
370 1997; Stanton & Rogelberg, 2001). Limited access calls into question the generalizability of the data to the overall population and can result in nonresponse bias.

To date, it is difficult to generalize the findings of most online research in FCS because most of the popu-
375 lations sampled are taken from a closed set (i.e., an e-mail directory or listserv). In other words, potential participants are not being selected from the entire population but instead, from a subset of the population that uses the Internet. (For further discussion, see
380 Moorefield & Proulx, 2004; and Litvin & Kar, 2001.) Kwon and Lee (2003) noted that, even though they used data from an Internet survey administered by a university research center, it was still difficult to generalize findings, even to the population of Internet users.
385 Travel market researchers, though, have had greater success than other FCS researchers. Litvin and Kar (2001) found that online survey respondents were significantly more likely to take vacation trips in the course of a year than the general population. As a re-
390 sult, the sample of online respondents was fairly representative of travelers in general. However, this study is not typical.

To address issues of generalizability and response bias, researchers need to obtain the highest possible
395 response rate for the population being sampled. Researchers also must consider oversampling from populations likely to be under-represented. A number of methods, including advance notices of the survey, reminders, and incentives, have been effectively used by
400 FCS researchers to boost online response rates and mitigate nonresponse bias. For example, Lyons (2003) contacted respondents using an e-mail "cover letter" that included a URL; students simply clicked on the URL to access the survey. She also sent three remind-
405 ers and provided students with a monetary incentive (vouchers to the university bookstore). Each reminder resulted in a significant increase in the number of student responses.

A personalized notice about the survey prior to its re-
410 lease also can dramatically improve response rates (i.e., Cook, Heath, & Thompson, 2000; Stanton & Rogelberg, 2001). According to Cook et al. (2000), the number of contacts, personalized contacts, and precontacts
415 are the dominant factors affecting response rates. In addition, many methodologists, including Dillman (2000), recommend sending three or more reminder e-mails. However, although reminders can increase response rates, researchers must be sensitive to their tar-
420 get populations and avoid sending multiple reminders that the participants might view as spam. Cook et al. (2000) found a slight decrease in response rates among those receiving two or more reminders. Lyons (2003) also found that two reminders were sufficient—although a third reminder increased the response rate, it
425 tended to be viewed by students as spam.

Although the preceding factors can affect response rates positively, other factors can influence response rates negatively. For example, with online surveys, the actual response environment cannot be controlled or
430 monitored by the researcher as it can be in a laboratory. While completing the survey, respondents outside a laboratory may be affected by random factors such as distractions at home or work or equipment and software difficulties. In addition, with online surveys, re-
435 searchers do not have physical and social interaction with the respondents, which can affect response rates, especially for experimental studies in child and family development and health and nutrition (i.e., Colvin et al., 2004; Daley et al., 2003; Selwyn & Robson, 1998).
440 Other factors related to the environment also can affect response rates negatively. For example, the same participant may submit surveys multiple times either intentionally or unintentionally. Also, the researcher may receive unsolicited responses from individuals
445 who were forwarded the invitation to participate in the study. Fortunately, safeguards can be implemented to verify the authenticity of responses. A website can be set up to use a cookie to obtain the IP address of the participant. The cookies, which are used to collect in-
450 formation for a particular website, can then be used to identify multiple submissions and remove them from the data set. However, participants and possibly a university's human subjects committee may find the use of cookies too intrusive. An alternative is to assign a
455 unique ID code to each e-mail using an e-mail management program. A website can be programmed to allow only one submission for each ID code.

Although the preceding techniques may help researchers boost response rates and reduce response
460 bias, it is still challenging, if not impossible, to calculate the actual response rates for online studies (Andrews et al., 2003). For example, a researcher may choose to post an invitation to participate in a survey on a company site. If the consumer is interested in par-
465 ticipating in the study, he or she can click on the invitation and go to the survey. Although it is possible to track the number of hits on a particular website, it is far more difficult to determine how many unique visitors there were to that site. It is even more difficult to assess
470 exactly who these consumers were demographically,

especially those who chose not to participate in the study.

If the invitation is posted on a website that the researchers do not control, they must rely on the host for data needed to calculate a response rate. Some companies or organizations may be unwilling to release this information because of concern that a competitor may use it to gain an advantage. For example, Cude and Morganosky (2000; Morganosky & Cude, 2002) secured the cooperation of an online grocer that was willing to post an invitation to participate in the survey after a consumer submitted an online grocery order. However, the researchers were unable to calculate a response rate because the online grocer would not provide information to them on the number of customers who purchased groceries online.

With respect to conducting online studies of students, researchers such as Lawrence et al. (2003) and Lyons (2003, 2004) were able to assess whether their samples were representative of the student populations as a whole. They were also able to obtain fairly accurate response rates because they knew, for the most part, how many students had been sent e-mail invitations to participate in the study. However, even in these cases, it was difficult for the researchers to determine exact response rates because of possible problems with the mailing lists such as multiple e-mail addresses for students and outdated addresses.

In the end, it is critical that researchers using online methodologies establish, to the best of their abilities, that their sample is representative of the population of interest and that every available means was used to secure the highest possible response rates. Only then can researchers assess whether an online survey is an effective means to collect data from their target populations.

Survey Design and Implementation

Once issues with the sample have been resolved, FCS researchers can begin to consider the design of their survey. Developing an online survey and setting up the website can require an extensive amount of work in the months prior to data collection. However, once the survey is posted, it can be completed, submitted, and downloaded into a central database in minutes. This section highlights the technical challenges researchers may face prior to launching a survey.

The majority of the discussion in this article has assumed that most researchers will post their survey to a website. However, a researcher may choose to send the survey as an attachment by e-mail. There are several issues to consider when choosing between an e-mail and an online survey. E-mail surveys might be useful if the researcher has a short turnaround time to complete the survey, the survey is short and simple in design, and/or the researcher does not have the technical expertise to design and implement an online survey. However, data collected from an e-mail survey must be manually entered into a database, unlike the automated data entry that results from an online survey. Whenever possible, more complex surveys should be implemented online rather than e-mailed because online surveys give the researcher more flexibility. Links, drop-down menus, and graphics can be used to help respondents navigate the survey, especially if the survey includes questions in which the answers are contingent on answers to earlier questions. Specifically, hyperlinks to the required questions can be used, a technique not possible in e-mail surveys because of differences in e-mail programs.

Fortunately, many of the principles of traditional survey design apply to online survey research as well. For example, as with any survey, it is critical that researchers think about their target audiences and how much time they are likely to spend on a survey. Higher response rates will be generated if messages and questionnaires are kept short. For example, Volpe et al. (2002) limited the amount of time online investors needed to complete their survey to 15 minutes, noting the busy schedules of investors. Obviously, the time restriction meant that the researchers had to be selective about the number and types of investment topics covered on the survey.

On the other hand, there are other opportunities and challenges that are unique to online survey methodology (see Dillman, 2000, for an overview). For example, in any survey the presentation and sequencing of questions are important because they can affect the quality of the data. A Web-based survey gives the researcher a broader choice of methods to reduce the probability that questions are skipped in error. However, with this said, Dillman (2000) recommended that researchers avoid requiring respondents to answer each question before they are allowed to move on to other questions. In addition, unless the order of the questions is a major concern, Dillman (2000) also recommended that the design of the survey should be flexible so that respondents can scroll quickly and easily from question to question to get a sense of the length of the survey and the types of questions being asked.

FCS researchers interested in collecting qualitative or "free-text" data may find online surveys to be particularly effective. Studies find that online surveys tend to result in more responses and longer responses to open-ended questions than is typical of traditional mail or telephone surveys (Bachmann el al., 2000; Cude & Morganosky, 2000; Joinson, 2001; Mehta & Sivades, 1995; Moorefield & Proulx, 2004; Oppermann, 1995). Other studies also show that the quality of responses to online surveys tends to be equal to or better than responses to other survey methods (i.e., Moorefield & Proulx, 2004; Tse, 1998). Joinson (2001), a behavioral science researcher, has shown how online surveys can increase the quantity of information individuals reveal about themselves. He found that the amount of information individuals reveal can be increased if the researcher also discloses personal information such as basic demographic information about himself or herself (i.e., a photograph, e-mail address, and telephone number).

590   There are two main advantages to collecting qualitative information online. First, software now exists that facilitates the coding by thematic content of the written responses to open-ended questions (Colvin et al., 2004; Hill et al., 1996). Second, if a researcher plans to use

595   software to analyze the qualitative data, the traditional first step—typing in the responses—is already completed.

Once critical questions about the survey design have been answered, researchers must consider the technical

600   challenges associated with posting the survey online. Researchers who lack the skills to post a survey online themselves have several options available. One approach is to look within their local campus or community for individuals who have the expertise and skills to

605   program the survey onto the Web. For example, a private market research firm, a campus-based Survey Research Center, or an undergraduate or graduate program in management information systems (or other related programs) are likely to include individuals who

610   have the skills to build an online survey. Professors and students in an undergraduate or a graduate program even may be looking for projects that the class or individual students in the class could complete. In addition, a project sponsor may have the resources to build an

615   online survey. For example, Hill et al. (1996) used IBM's existing Online Opinion Survey (OOS) program. The OOS program could be accessed by employees from IBM's mainframe computer network and had built-in error checks that notified the respondent if

620   an invalid response had been entered.

Another approach is to use one of several different websites available to build a Web-based survey. A variety of software tools are now available on these sites. The tools are becoming increasingly sophisticated yet

625   at the same time easy to use. A few of the sites include www.surveymonkey.com, www.surveypro.com, www.infopoll.com, www.zoomerang.com, and www.ultrafeedback.com. A feature of many of the websites is that they allow the researcher to obtain minute-by-

630   minute updates and reports on survey responses and response rates to each survey question. Essentially, researchers can instantaneously view the results as soon as any respondent has completed the survey. All of the sites offer basic services at no cost and/or dis-

635   counts for educational and nonprofit organizations. Pricing generally varies with the number of questions, the number of responses, and the sophistication of the design options. For example, the recent price for one service was $19.95 per month for up to 1,000 re-

640   sponses; another was charging $499 for 3 months for 1,000 responses.

Once the survey is designed, it is of critical importance that researchers test the survey before it is

645   launched to ensure that it is working properly and the responses entered are being collected and stored. It is fairly common for technical difficulties to arise when an online survey is first launched. Web browsers and settings can vary by user, and these differences can affect the appearance of the online survey. There also

650   may be incompatibilities among different systems (i.e., different screen configurations or operating systems) or difficulties with the server (Andrews et al., 2003; Dillman, 2000; Stanton & Rogelberg, 2001). Researchers must be prepared to address technical issues quickly.

655   Also, survey respondents need to know who they can contact if they have difficulty accessing the survey or questions about the study. To minimize variations in survey appearance and system incompatibilities, researchers may want to design an online survey that

660   does not exceed the "lowest common denominator" of computer sophistication and complexity (i.e., monitor size, browser version) of the target population being surveyed (Wharton et al., 2003).

Data Storage, Privacy, and Confidentiality

665   Once an online survey has been developed and tested, it is ready to be posted to the website. The critical questions researchers need to ask before it is launched are: Where will the data that are entered be downloaded and how will they be stored? The website

670   where the survey is posted must be on a server that has the capabilities to download and store the data.

In most cases, researchers may be able to rely on their campus or other organization to provide this service, using their own server for little or no cost. How-

675   ever, researchers may also want to look for hidden or in-kind resources to host the survey from either their own organization or a project sponsor (i.e., private firm, Survey Research Center, or other partner). For example, a project sponsor may have a substantial Web

680   division that is capable of hosting the survey and storing the data on a local data server, resulting in lower survey instrumentation costs. The researcher's organization or the group or organization that built the online survey may have the resources to host the survey and

685   store the data. Finally, an advantage of using a website such as surveymonkey.com or surveypro.com to build an online survey is that the website will host the survey and store the data, which the researchers may download at any time.

690   Whichever direction researchers choose to take, the survey needs to be set up so that the data are collected using an appropriate database. Selection of the database depends, in part, on whether the data are quantitative or qualitative. For example, more qualitative re-

695   sponses require larger amounts of storage space. Once the data are stored, the information typically can be transferred to the researcher in multiple methods. One such method would be a regular digest that is e-mailed to the researcher; this could be daily or weekly. There

700   also can be a download-on-demand feature as well as

using file transfer protocol with the host server. These downloads can be in ASCII text format or even Microsoft Excel spreadsheets. Either of these formats can be imported into most statistical analysis programs such as 705 SAS and SPSS.

Given consumer privacy issues, researchers also must ensure that the data being entered are downloaded and stored on a secure server. One of the most common methods used by researchers to secure the data as they 710 are collected is to use an encryption method to design the Web pages where information is gathered and sent to the database. There are different levels of encryption; the current standard is 128-bit Secure Socket Layer encryption. Encrypted data can be opened only 715 by the appropriate machines and are useless to anyone intercepting the data during its transit from one server to another (Department of Treasury, n.d.).

Several steps can be taken to secure the server(s) on which the data are stored and protect the data from 720 potential hackers or those with unauthorized access. Access to the data can be limited to certain machines and require a password for access (Andrews et al., 2003). For example, Colvin et al. (2004) housed their survey on a secure server that could be accessed only 725 by the primary researcher via a user name and password. Using Macromedia Dreamweaver 3 software and FrontPage, no identifying information such as e-mail addresses or Web routing numbers were transported with the survey when it was submitted. Any survey that 730 is connected to the Internet also should be protected from potential hackers through the use of a firewall. A firewall is a software program that determines which packets of information can get to or from the computer or network; it can prevent outside users from accessing 735 the data (SearchSecurity.com, n.d.).

Once the data entry process is secured, researchers must communicate to the target population the steps they have taken to protect respondents' anonymity and confidentiality so that they feel comfortable providing 740 and submitting information online. Although researchers increasingly are using online surveys, it is still likely that many potential respondents may be completing a survey online for the first time. Those populations that lack experience are likely to be more sensitive to 745 the issue of consumer privacy. For example, researchers have found that women and older adults have greater concerns about personal privacy than do men and younger individuals (Dommeyer & Gross, 2003). Groups that are more experienced with the Internet 750 typically have fewer concerns about online privacy issues. These groups, such as online shoppers, investors, and students, typically are more experienced in using remote purchasing methods (i.e., mail order) and completing transactions online (Miyazaki & Fernandez, 2001). 755

Regardless of the level of experience, response rates are likely to be higher if researchers are able to provide assurance that measures are in place to protect participant privacy and anonymity. Cho and LaRose (1999) 760 provided researchers with a variety of measures that can be used to address privacy concerns related to online surveys. These include separating the consent form from the survey, compensating for the privacy intrusion by offering incentives, collecting data through 765 Web pages (to separate respondents' e-mail addresses from the data), and offering alternative ways to respond (see also Stanton & Rogelberg, 2001). Researchers who plan to collect data from some groups, such as employees or military personnel, may find that online 770 surveys are inappropriate, especially if researchers are unable to provide adequate assurance that the employer will not have access to the information being collected.

In addition to providing assurance to their respondents, researchers also need to provide assurance and 775 obtain approval to conduct their study from their institutional review board that protects human subjects (i.e., Im & Chee, 2002; Stanton & Rogelberg, 2001). It is critical that researchers set aside an appropriate amount of time to obtain approval on their campus or else- 780 where before the study is conducted. Often, researchers underestimate the amount of time it will take to obtain human subjects' approval, especially for an online study, as these studies present special issues related to data security and confidentiality. Researchers should be 785 aware that they may be asked to provide more instruction and orientation to respondents than they otherwise would need to with an oral or written survey instrument. In addition, if a company or organization has agreed to provide access to an e-mail list or online di- 790 rectory of members or to post an invitation to participate on a website, that entity also may request or require the opportunity to review the survey before the study can be conducted. The bottom line is that researchers need to plan early when using an online sur- 795 vey because a significant amount of preparation and technical assistance may be required to ensure the anonymity and confidentiality of the respondents.

Conclusion

As online access continues to grow, so too will the 800 use of online surveys in FCS research. As with any data collection tool, one must consider the pros and cons. The challenges associated with online surveying range from increasing survey response rates and improving sample representativeness to survey design, 805 confidentiality, and data storage. (See again the flowchart in Table 1 to review the process for conducting an online survey.) Researchers who have not previously conducted an online study may be unaware of some of the challenges as well as the time and costs 810 required for implementation. For example, unlike mail surveys, the oversight of the actual data collection can be time-consuming. In addition, unlike traditional mail or telephone surveys, a significant amount of time must be invested before an online study is launched. In par- 815 ticular, a substantial amount of infrastructure must be in place before the survey can be posted online. Before opting to conduct an online survey, researchers should consider the objective(s) of the study, the target population, and their available resources.

820   With this said, online surveys can be a powerful data collection tool. The numerous benefits associated with the use of online surveys include larger sample sizes, faster response times, less data processing, and lower marginal costs. Researchers in FCS are increasingly

825 turning to online surveys because, once a survey is completed, the data can be downloaded quickly into a database for analysis, eliminating the need for data entry, which can be time- and resource-intensive.

    Yet FCS researchers must be aware of the challenges

830 that lie ahead as the use of online surveys continues. As their uniqueness begins to fade, online survey response rates are likely to decline. New incentives may be needed to generate interest and encourage continued participation in online studies. Also, because online

835 surveying is still relatively new to FCS, editors, reviewers, and others who evaluate research may not be familiar with the techniques, especially with respect to the challenges associated with the generalizability of the findings. As more research is conducted using

840 online surveying methods, researchers will have a better sense of how to evaluate the validity of this type of research and its contributions to the field. In the meantime, this article lays a foundation by providing insight into the opportunities and challenges that FCS re-

845 searchers are likely to face when conducting online survey research. A number of excellent resources and examples from FCS have been cited that serve as a starting point to any investigator who wants to learn more about online surveying techniques.

References

Anderson, R. M., Donnelly, M. B., & Hess, G. E. (1992). An assessment of computer use, knowledge, and attitudes of diabetes educators. *Diabetes Education, 18*(1), 40–46.

Andrews, D., Nonnecke, B., & Preece, J. (2003). Electronic survey methodology: A case study in reaching hard-to-involve Internet users. *International Journal of Human-Computer Interaction, 16*(2), 185–210.

Bachmann, D. P., Elfrink, J., & Vazzana, G. (2000). E-mail and snail mail face off in rematch. *Marketing Research, 11*(4), 10–15.

Baruch, Y. (1999). Response rates in academic studies: A comparative analysis. *Human Relations, 52*(4), 421–434.

Birnbaum, M. H. (2004). Human research and data collection via the Internet. *Annual Review of Psychology, 55*(1), 803–832.

Cho, H., & LaRose, R. (1999). Privacy issues in Internet surveys. *Social Science Computer Review, 17*(4), 421–434.

Cobanoglu, C., Warde, B., & Moreo, P. J. (2001). A comparison of mail, fax, and Web-based survey methods. *International Journal of Market Research, 43*(4), 441–452.

Colvin, J., Chenoweth, L., Bold, M., & Harding, C. (2004). Caregivers of older adults: Advantages and disadvantages of Internet-based social support. *Family Relations, 53*(1), 49–57.

Cook, C., Heath, F., & Thompson, R. L. (2000). A meta-analysis of response rates in Web- or Internet-based surveys. *Educational and Psychological Measurement, 60*(6), 821–836.

Cooper, A., Morahan-Martin, J., Mathy, R. M., & Maheu, M. (2002). Toward an increased understanding of user demographics in online sexual activities. *Journal of Sex & Marital Therapy, 28*, 105–129.

Cude, B. J., & Morganosky, M. (2000). Consumer response to online grocery shopping. *International Journal of Retail and Distribution Management, 28*, 17–26.

Daley, E., McDermott, R., McCormack-Brown, K., & Kittleson, M. (2003). Conducting Web-based survey research: A lesson in Internet designs. *American Journal of Health Behavior, 27*(2), 116–124.

Department of Treasury. (n.d.). *128 bit Secure Sockets Layer (SSL) encryption.* Retrieved May 1, 2004, from http://www.michigan.gov/treasury/0%2C1607 %2C7-121-1750_17289-52359—%2C00.html

Dillman, D. A. (2000). Mail and Internet surveys: *The tailored design method* (2nd ed.). New York: John Wiley.

Dommeyer, C. J., & Gross, B. L. (2003). What consumers know and what they do: An investigation of consumer knowledge, awareness, and use of privacy protection strategies. *Journal of Interactive Marketing, 17*(2), 34–51.

Farris, N. A., Stoupa, R. A., Mendenhall, J. D., & Mazzuca, K. B. (1994). A computerized education module for documenting patient outcomes. *Computers in Nursing, 12*(6), 272–276.

Gosling, S. D., Vazire, S., & Srivastava, S. (2004). Should we trust Web-based studies? A comparative analysis of six preconceptions about Internet questionnaires. *American Psychologist, 59*(2), 93–104.

Hanna, S. D., Gutter, M. S., & Fan, J. X. (2001). A measure of risk tolerance based on economic theory. *Financial Counseling and Planning, 12*, 53–60.

Hill, E. J., Hawkins, H. J., & Miller, B. C. (1996). Work and family in the virtual office: Perceived influences on mobile telework. *Family Relations, 45*(31), 293–301.

Im, E., & Chee, W. (2002). Issues in protection of human subjects in Internet research. *Nursing Research, 51*, 266–269.

Jackson, A., & DeCormier, R. (1999). E-mail survey response rates: Targeting increases response. *Marketing Intelligence & Planning, 17*(3), 135–139.

Joinson, A. (2001). Knowing me, knowing you: Reciprocal self-disclosure in Internet-based surveys. *Cyber Psychology & Behavior, 4*, 587–591.

Katz, J., & Aspden, P. (1997). Motivations and barriers to Internet usage: Results of a national public opinion survey. *Internet Research: Electronic Networking Applications and Policy, 7*(3), 170–188.

Kwon, K. N., & Lee, J. (2003). Concerns about payment security of Internet purchases: A perspective on current on-line shoppers. *Clothing and Textiles Research Journal, 21*(4), 174–184.

Lawrence, F. C., Christofferson, R. C., Nester, S., Moser, B., Tucker, J. A., & Lyons, A. C. (2003). *Credit card usage of college students: Evidence from Louisiana State University* (Research Information Sheet No. 107). Baton Rouge: Louisiana State University, Agricultural Center.

Lenhart, A. (2003, April 16). *The ever-shifting Internet population: A new look at Internet access and the digital divide.* Retrieved September 15, 2003, from http://www.pewinternet.org/reports/pdfs/PIP_Shifting_Net_Pop_Report.pdf

Litvin, S. W., & Kar, G. H. (2001). E-surveying for tourism research: Legitimate tool or a researcher's fantasy? *Journal of Travel Research, 39*(3), 308.

Lyons, A. C. (2003). *The credit usage and financial education needs of Midwest college students* (Report to Midwest College Administrators). Urbana/Champaign: University of Illinois at Urbana-Champaign.

Lyons, A. C. (2004). A profile of financially at-risk college students. *Journal of Consumer Affairs, 38*(1), 56–80.

McDonald, H., & Adam, S. (2003). A comparison of online and postal data collection methods in marketing research. *Marketing Intelligence & Planning, 21*(2), 85–95.

McKay, H. G., King, D., Eakin, E. G., Seeley, J. R., & Glasgow, R. E. (2001). The Diabetes Network Internet-Based Physical Activity Intervention: A randomized pilot study. *Diabetes Care, 24*(8), 1328–1334.

Meadows, K. A., Fromson, B., Gillespie, C., Brewer, A., Carter, C., Lockington, T., et al. (1988). Development, validation, and application of computer-linked knowledge questionnaires in diabetes education. *Diabetic Medicine, 5*(1), 61–67.

Mehta, R., & Sivades, E. (1995). Comparing response rates and response content in mail versus electronic mail surveys. *Journal of the Market Research Society, 37*(4), 429–439.

Miyazaki, A. D., & Fernandez, A. (2001). Consumer perceptions of privacy and security risks for online shopping. *Journal of Consumer Affairs, 35*(1), 27–44.

Moorefield, B. S., & Proulx, C. M. (2004, November). *Couple identity and couple-verification: Extending identity theory to gay male couples and families.* Discussion paper at the 33rd Theory Construction and Research Methodology Workshop, Vancouver, Canada.

Morganosky, M. A., & Cude, B. J. (2002). Consumer demand for online food retailing: Is it really a supply side issue? *International Journal of Retail and Distribution Management, 30*, 451–458.

Murray, D., & Fisher, J. (2002). The Internet: A virtually untapped tool for research. *Journal of Technology in Human Services, 19*(2/3), 5–18.

Nosek, B. A., Banaji, M. R., & Greenwald, A. G. (2002). E-research: Ethics, security, design, and control in psychological research on the Internet. *Journal of Social Issues, 58*(1), 161–177.

Oppermann, M. (1995). E-mail surveys—potentials and pitfalls. *Marketing Research, 7*, 29–33.

Pollack, S., Foster, K., & Robinson, V. (2004). *Making the financial grade: The state of personal financial knowledge and credit card use among freshmen and sophomore college students in Georgia*. Athens: University of Georgia, Carl Vinson Institute of Government.

Reips, U. (2002). Internet-based psychological experimenting: Five do's and don'ts. *Social Science Computer Review, 20*, 241–249.

SearchSecurity.com. (n.d.). *Firewall*. Retrieved May 1, 2004, from http://searchsecurity.techtarget.com/sDefinition/0%2C%2Csid14_gci21212 5%2C00.html

Selwyn, N., & Robson, K. (1998). Using e-mail as a research tool. *Social Research Update*. Retrieved June 20, 2004, from http://www.soc.surrey.ac. uk/sru/SRU21.html

Solomon, D. J. (2001). Conducting Web-based surveys. *Practical Assessment, Research & Evaluation, 7*(19). Retrieved June 20, 2004, from http://PAREonline.net

Stanton, J. M., & Rogelberg, S. G. (2001). Research methods and the Internet using Internet/Intranet Web pages to collect organizational research data. *Organizational Research Methods, 4*(3), 200–217.

Taylor, H. (2000). Does Internet research work? *International Journal of Market Research, 42*(1), 51–63.

Tse, A. C. B. (1998). Comparing the response rate, response speed, and response quality of two methods of sending questionnaires: E-mail vs. mail. *Journal of the Market Research Society, 40*(4), 353–362.

UCLA Center for Communication Policy. (2003). *The UCLA Internet Report: Survey the digital future—Year three*. Retrieved January 7, 2004, from http://ccp.ucla.edu/pdf/UCLA-Internet-Report-Year-Three.pdf

Vereecken, C. (2001). Paper pencil versus PC administered querying of a study on health behaviour in school-aged children. *Archives of Public Health, 59*(1), 43–61.

Volpe, R. P., Kotel, J. E., & Chen, H. (2002). A survey of investment literacy among online investors. *Financial Counseling and Planning, 13*, 1–13.

Wharton, C., Hampl, J. S., Hall, R., & Winham, D. M. (2003). PCs or paper and pencil: Online surveys for data collection. *Journal of American Dietetic Association, 103*(11), 1458, 1460.

Wilson, A., & Laskey, N. (2003). Internet based marketing research: A serious alternative to traditional research methods? *Marketing Intelligence & Planning, 21*(2), 79–84.

Notes:

Notes: